S.V.R. MUSEUM
KIDDERMINSTER.
May '92
(B'DAY GIFT
FROM PAT.).

BOOK SALE £5.95.

METROPOLITAN STEAM LOCOMOTIVES

METROPOLITAN
STEAM LOCOMOTIVES

FRANK GOUDIE

Capital Transport

ISBN 185414 118 X

Published by Capital Transport Publishing
38 Long Elmes, Harrow Weald, Middlesex

Printed by Winchmore Press Ltd
Fowler Road, Hainault, Ilford, Essex

Title page *C Class* 0-4-4T No.69, built by Neilson & Co in 1891, at Finchley Road in the mid-1890s. Next to the engine is a four-wheeled brake van; the stubby signals and the signalbox are of typical Metropolitan design. No.69 was sold in 1923 to Charles Williams of Morriston, Glamorgan. Author's collection

Opposite **Summer in Metro-Land.** *H Class* 4-4-4T No.107 in a sylvan setting near Chorley Wood on an Aylesbury train, circa 1930. Built by Kerr Stuart in 1921 at a cost of £11,575 and sold to the LNER in 1937, it became *LNER Class H2* No.6419. In December 1941 it was transferred to Colwick shed, Nottingham, and was withdrawn in September 1943.

Contents

Introduction

The Metropolitan Railway had several claims to be unique among the underground railways of London. Due to the influence of Sir Edward Watkin, its Chairman from 1872 to 1894, it boasted a main line stretching far out into the rural reaches of Buckinghamshire – a result of Watkin's scheme to link up with the Great Central's London extension; its Brill branch, a single-track byway which ended some distance from the tiny village it purposed to serve, was a startling contrast with the murky tunnels of the Inner Circle. It also possessed horse boxes, milk vans, two Pullman cars, and a fairly extensive freight traffic. In the era of electric underground railways the Met continued to use steam traction on its outer suburban services. Indeed, this use of steam traction lasted from 1864, when the first Beyer Peacock 4-4-0 tanks entered service, until 1964, when the last Met steam locomotive, E Class 0-4-4-T No.1, was withdrawn as London Transport's L44, and so spanned a century.

My own acquaintance with the Metropolitan dates from the late 1920s when, as a small boy, I lived at Amersham. The handsome 4-4-4 tanks hauling varnished teak 'Dreadnought' coaches were a familiar sight, as were the G Class 0-6-4 tanks and K Class 2-6-4Ts, both types usually seen on goods train duties. In the afternoons a pick-up goods train, worked by a K Class engine, used to call at Amersham, and spent some time shunting and marshalling its train in the goods yard. Watching this operation, I was puzzled by a strange noise which occasionally came from the engine. In those days my technical knowledge was very limited, and it was many years before I discovered that this was the sound of the super-heater header discharge valve working. Still later, a working timetable told me that this was the No.3 Goods Train which left Verney Junction at 8.10am and, after shunting all the goods yards en route, finally arrived at Harrow at 9.40pm – a *pick-up* goods train indeed!

E Class 0-4-4 tanks were familiar performers on the Chesham branch, and an F Class 0-6-2T occasionally appeared on an engineer's train.

The Met & Great Central Joint line was full of interest in those days. Manchester expresses were hauled by ex-GC 'Director' Class 4-4-0s and 'Atlantics', while the suburban trains of Robinson's very comfortable match-board-panelled suburban coaches were worked by ex-Great Central 4-6-2 tanks of LNER Class A5. The 3.20pm express from Marylebone, charging through Amersham behind a 'Director', was a stirring sight indeed.

One day while walking home from school I saw, standing on a ballast train at Amersham, a very strange beast. It had closely-spaced bogie wheels, a tiny coal bunker inside the cab, and long pipes running from outside its cylinders to the side tanks. A sloping smokebox door, horizontally hinged, completed its exotic appearance. At this time I did not even know of the existence of the famous Beyer Peacock 4-4-0 tanks, and I gazed with amazement on this strange looking machine.

But these early experiences were the foundation of my affection for the Metropolitan Railway, a feeling which has developed over the years. If I have succeeded in conveying some of this enthusiasm in this book I shall be well satisfied.

Researching and writing it has been a very enjoyable task, made more so by the generous help I have received from many people. Among these I would mention Philip Atkins, Librarian of the National Railway Museum, York, whose article in the magazine 'Railways South East' for Winter 1987/88 brought to light much new information on the design of Met locomotives and who has helped in other ways; Robert Barker, for help regarding Neasden Works and engine sheds and the smaller Met engines; Geoffrey Horsman of Hunslet (Holdings) PLC, who hold the records of Kerr, Stuart & Co, for information regarding the 4-4-4 tank engines built for the Met, and my brother Ken, who checked the proofs. I am also grateful to the Greater London Record Office and to the Public Record Office at Kew for facilities to consult Metropolitan Railway and LNER archives. To those organisations and individuals who provided photographs for illustrations I would also like to express my appreciation; acknowledgement is made in the captions.

Eltham, London, March 1990 FRANK GOUDIE

'Fowler's Ghost' on a trial trip by the Stafford Street (now Conway Street) bridge at Edgware Road, 24th May 1862. Note mixed gauge track; the rails in the foreground appear to be temporary contractor's lines. This was one of a series of trials of the locomotive which took place between October 1861 and 1865 on the Great Western and on the Metropolitan itself. The livery appears to have been dark green, with cylinder cladding, splashers, footplate valance, wheels and steps dark Indian red. Smokebox, chimney, footplate and underframe were black, with footplate sidesheets and tender back and sides panelled in orange chrome, thinly lined in black. London Transport Museum

1 **The Early Years**

The Metropolitan Railway, opened from Bishops Road, Paddington to Farringdon Street on 10th January 1863, was the first underground railway in the world. Under its Act of Parliament it was required to provide locomotives which would not emit steam or smoke – an impossible condition, but a great deal of thought was given to the problem. John (later Sir John) Fowler, the Metropolitan's Engineer, at first proposed using locomotives with no fire but with a reservoir of hot water under pressure which could be heated up at the end of each journey, together with a reservoir of cold water in which the steam could condense – in other words, a fireless locomotive. In thinking this was a feasible method of working he was supported by Brunel.

But by 1860 Fowler had devised a modified scheme, and a locomotive was ordered from Robert Stephenson & Co. This was the famous 'Fowler's Ghost', an unofficial name, but a very appropriate one, for it was a failure and some of its history is still shrouded in mystery. It was equipped with a small firebox and a large quantity of firebricks in a chamber in the boiler barrel. The idea was to run it as an ordinary locomotive on open sections of line with full blast, thus getting the firebricks white hot, so that they would serve as a heat reservoir in the tunnel sections, where the fire was damped down and thus, in theory, avoiding emission of smoke. The exhaust steam was discharged into an injection-type condenser fitted with an air pump. The engine was a 2-4-0 tender locomotive, with 5ft 6in coupled wheels and outside cylinders 15 inches in diameter with 24 inch stroke. It cost £4,500, a high figure compared with the first Beyer Peacock 4-4-0 tanks which the Metropolitan purchased in 1864, which cost only £2,675.

In October it was taken out onto the Great Western Railway for trials (it was a broad gauge engine; the Metropolitan was initially worked by the GWR).

After running for 7½ miles as an ordinary locomotive it was turned ready for the return journey. The fire was shut off and the exhaust steam was discharged into the condensing tanks. But after 12 minutes the condensing apparatus was so hot that steam was coming out of the air pump delivery pipe mixed with boiling water. Boiler pressure fell from 120lb per square inch to 80lb, and the firebricks had cooled to the point where they were almost black. After a feed-pump failure, the fire was dropped, and thus ended the first trial run. At least one further trial was apparently held, however, this time on the Metropolitan itself, as a photograph exists showing it between Kings Cross and Edgware Road, probably in 1862.

It was quite a handsome engine, with a bell-mouthed chimney, safety valves on the dome, which was just behind the chimney, open splashers, a weatherboard bent slightly back at the top, and a four-wheeled tender. Any trials over the Metropolitan would presumably have been even less successful than the one on the GWR, as there were only very short open sections between Bishops Road and Farringdon Street, so the 'Ghost' would have had little chance of working as a normal engine and heating the firebricks to the temperature necessary to raise steam in the tunnel sections. The engine then lay derelict at Hammersmith until 1865, when the chassis and engine portions, but not the boiler, were purchased by Isaac Watt Boulton, where they languished at his yard at Ashton-under-Lyne until the firm closed. The remains were sold to Beyer-Peacock and cannibalised.

Stephenson's prepared an amended design in 1861, for a 4-2-2ST, with 200lb boiler pressure, and a saddle tank above two boiler barrels, but this was never built.

'Fowler's Ghost' 2-4-0T on the inspection trip at Edgware Road, 24th May 1862. A similar photograph, more widely published and retouched to show part of the locomotive, has led to the incorrect surmise that the loco was one of the contractor's engines. The party includes W.E. Gladstone (who was then Chancellor of the Exchequer) and his wife, and John Fowler, the Engineer (in light coloured top hat, leaning on side of wagon). The initials 'S & K' stand for Smith & Knight, who were the contractors for the Bishops Road to Gower Street section of the railway. NRM

Following the failure of 'Fowler's Ghost' it fell to Daniel Gooch, Locomotive Superintendent of the Great Western, to design locomotives to work the Metropolitan line. He chose a broad gauge 2-4-0 tank with outside cylinders 16ins by 24ins, 160lb boiler pressure, and weighing 45 tons in working order. They had domeless boilers 10ft 6ins long and 4ft 9ins in diameter, and were without cabs. The outside cylinders, unusual for a broad gauge engine but necessary to leave room between the frames for condensing tanks, sloped steeply. The first six engines were built by the Vulcan Foundry and were named after insects, 'Mosquito', 'Hornet' etc. The second six, from Kitson & Co, received names of foreign potentates, such as 'Czar', 'Mogul' etc. These twelve locomotives were delivered in time for the opening of the line on 10th January 1863. Later a further ten were built at Swindon, and named after flowers. They dealt with the Metropolitan traffic very successfully, though the condensing apparatus gave rise to some problems. The coaches were 8-wheeled Great Western vehicles known as 'Long Charleys', with gas lighting and seating 49.

Great enthusiasm was shown by the public on opening day and large crowds patronised the trains; at one time booking at Kings Cross had to be suspended for an hour, and 40,000 tickets were issued that day.

But disagreements soon arose between GWR and the Metropolitan. The latter company wanted a more frequent service than the four trains an hour which Charles Saunders, the GWR Secretary and General Superintendent, considered to be the limit that could be safely worked. The Great Western, for their part, were aggrieved because the Metropolitan refused to let them subscribe to shares in the extension to Moorgate. As the Great Western had contributed £175,000 to the Metropolitan's original capital, they felt they were entitled to purchase shares in the extension, which were selling at a premium. They applied to the Court of Chancery to support their entitlement to subscribe to a proportion of these shares, but the Vice-Chancellor ruled against them.

Relations between the two companies were now very strained, and the Metropolitan Board instructed Sir John Fowler on 6th May to consider the best way of working the railway in the event of a rupture with the Great Western. This soon came; on 18th July the GWR gave notice that they would cease to work the Metropolitan services at the end of September. The Metropolitan replied that they

Great Western Railway broad gauge 2-4-0 tank engine 'Locust', one of 22 engines designed by Daniel Gooch for working Metropolitan train services on the opening of the line from Bishops Road to Farringdon Street. This was one of the first six engines of the type, built in 1862 by the Vulcan Foundry; the second six were by Kitsons of Leeds, and the last ten were constructed at Swindon. They were unusual for their time in having outside cylinders and were probably the first GWR engines with this feature; this was necessary in order to obtain plenty of space between the frames for condensing tanks. After the Met obtained its own 4-4-0 tank engines from Beyer Peacock, these Great Western machines continued to appear on the Metropolitan, hauling GWR trains from Windsor to Farringdon Street.
Loco Publishing Company

Great Western Railway broad gauge train on the Metropolitan Railway near Paddington in 1863, showing one of the twenty-two 2-4-0 well tanks designed by Daniel Gooch for Met service. LT Museum

would take over the operation of the line themselves on 30th September. Whereupon Saunders said that the GWR would withdraw its trains on 10th August. They evidently expected that this would force the Metropolitan to capitulate, but Fowler reported that he had arranged for the Great Northern Railway to loan suitable locomotives and rolling stock so that the Metropolitan could work the service themselves when the GWR trains were withdrawn.

So on the morning of 11th August the Met were ready to carry on 'business as usual'. The Metropolitan had, fortunately, been laid with mixed broad and standard gauge rails in order that the Great Northern, who had a connection with the Metropolitan at Kings Cross, could run a train service to Farringdon Street. Sturrock, the GNR Locomotive Superintendent and, ironically enough, an old Swindon man, fitted up some rather aged 0-4-2 and 0-6-0 tender engines with condensing apparatus. These took over the Metropolitan train service on August 11th, hauling coaches borrowed from the GNR and the LNWR. There were some problems at first with the narrow gauge rails, which had never been tested, and on 9th May 1864 GNR No.138, an 0-6-0 built by R. & W. Hawthorn in 1850, exploded at Bishops Road when the top of the middle ring of the boiler blew off, injuring the crew and a brakesman who was standing on the platform. But apart from these incidents the Great Northern engines seem to have worked the service quite adequately.

But the Metropolitan realised that they would have to obtain their own locomotives and rolling stock and, as described in Chapter 2, this paved the way for the most famous of the Metropolitan engines, the 4-4-0 tanks built by Beyer Peacock.

By the autumn tempers had cooled and the two companies had settled their differences, with the result that the Great Western began working a passenger service from Windsor to Farringdon Street and later, after the extension to Moorgate was opened in 1865, to the latter point. They also operated goods trains over the Metropolitan, using, until the broad gauge vanished from the Met in March 1869, six 0-6-0 tank engines built at Swindon in 1866 to the design of Joseph Armstrong. These had 17in by 24in cylinders and coupled wheels 4ft 6in in diameter, and one of them was named 'Fowler' in honour of the Metropolitan's Engineer. After the end of broad gauge on the Met they were transferred to the West Country, where some of them were rebuilt as saddle tanks.

B Class 4-4-0T No.59 on a Rickmansworth train, composed of Jubilee stock 4-wheeled coaches, near Northwood circa 1900. The engine has a cast-iron chimney and covered-in slide bars as fitted by T.F. Clark, but still retains spring balance safety valves on the dome. Together with Nos.57 and 58, this locomotive was delivered when new (1880) to the South Eastern Railway, becoming SER No.301. It was returned to the Metropolitan three years later. LGRP

2 The Beyer Peacock 4-4-0 Tank Engines

As already related, after the dispute with the Great Western led to that company deciding to cease working the Metropolitan train services beyond 10th August 1863, the Great Northern lent locomotives for this purpose. The Metropolitan board realised that they would have to take over these workings themselves, and on 21st July Sir John Fowler, the Engineer, was instructed to obtain tenders for suitable locomotives and carriages. On 7th October a tender was received from Beyer Peacock of Manchester for building new engines at £2,600 each, and Fowler was authorised to accept the tender for 18 engines, which he said should be ready in six months time.

The design of these famous 4-4-0 tank engines has often been attributed to Sir John Fowler, but R.H. Burnett, of Beyer Peacock, said that Fowler only specified driving wheel diameter, weight per axle, and suitability for sharp curves. The working out of detailed design was left to Beyer Peacock, and the Metropolitan engines were, in fact, a development of a 4-4-0 tank engine which Beyers had built for the Tudela & Bilbao Railway in Spain. These had cylinders 16in by 20in, coupled wheels 5ft 0½in diameter, and weighed 38.1 tons in working order. They had Bissell trucks, in which the four-wheeled bogie, on a polished plane bearing surface, was pivoted on a girder, which joined the frames just in front of the driving wheels. The outside cylinders sloped backwards at about 1 in 7½.

When it came to working out the details for the Metropolitan engines the Tudela & Bilbao Railway design was taken as a basis. A major part in the design of the Spanish locomotives had been taken by Thomas Hunt, the Tudela & Bilbao's first locomotive superintendent, so much of the credit for designing the Met engines should go to him. The Metropolitan locomotives were larger, with cylinders 17in by 24in and 5ft 9in coupled wheels. Instead of the closed dome and Ramsbottom safety-valves of the Spanish engines, the Met machines had domes with spring balance valves on the first ring of the

A *Class 4-4-0T No.44*, as built in 1869, with sandbox on boiler behind dome, and wooden brake blocks. This engine was sold to Pelaw Main Colliery in 1926 via R. Fraser of Newcastle-on-Tyne, and survived until 1948. Loco Publishing Co

boiler; the Bissell trucks were retained. Cylinders sloped more steeply at 1 in 9, and Allan straight-link motion was fitted. Characteristic Beyer Peacock copper-capped chimneys and polished brass domes set off the light green livery nicely. Condensing apparatus was fitted, controlled by valves over the cylinders from which copper pipes led the steam into the side tanks; these valves were operated by levers linked by a rod to the footplate control. Sandboxes, delivering sand in front of the driving wheels, were originally on top of the boilers behind the dome. There was no cab, only a spectacle-plate, and the bunkers were small, carrying only 40 cubic feet of coal, though this was increased in later engines. Weight in working order of the first 18 engines was 42 tons 3cwt.

These engines, Met. Nos.1 to 18 and Beyer Peacock Works Nos.412 to 429, were delivered in 1864, and received names from Greek mythology carried on brass plates fixed to the sides of the boilers, but these names were removed as the engines came in for overhaul. Two years later Nos.19 to 23 were delivered (Works Nos.706 to 710). Subsequent engines were built as follows:–

Met. No.	Works No.	Built
24-28	770-774	1867
29-33	853-857	1868
39-44	863-868	1869

Nos.19 to 33 and 39 to 44 had the same dimensions as the original batch of engines except that they had larger coal bunkers. Nos.1 to 33 and 39 to 44 were later known as Class 'A'.

Five similar locomotives, Nos. 45-49 (Works Nos.893-897 were delivered in 1870). In 1879 a modified design, Class 'B', was introduced by Joseph Tomlinson, who had succeeded Burnett as Locomotive Superintendent. These had Adams bogies instead of Bissell trucks, and larger tanks than Class 'A'.

Several dimensions were altered (a full list of dimensions appears at the end of this chapter). A double pipe led from the lock-up safety-valves on the firebox to the tank tops, so that blow-off steam was carried into the water space (some 'A' Class engines also had this feature). The 'B' Class engines were built as follows:–

Met Nos.	Works Nos.	Built
34-38	1878-1882	1879-1880
50-59	1937-1940, 1944-1946, 1941-1943	1880
60-64	2579-2583	1884
65-66	2674-2675	1885

A *Class* 4-4-0T No.18, last of the initial batch of Beyer Peacock engines delivered in 1864. In original condition, it carries its nameplate, 'Hercules', though this was later removed and subsequent engines of the series did not receive names. The livery is light olive green with yellow lining though, possibly because of the limitations of photographic plates in those days, the latter does not show in this view. What appear to be clerestories on the coaches are, in fact, collapsible containers for the coal gas used for lighting. Note the track with ballast almost up to rail level. Real Photographs

Nos.34 to 38 took the numbers previously carried by the five 0-6-0 tank engines built by the Worcester Engine Co, which had been sold in 1868. The last two 'B' Class engines, Nos.65 and 66, were not delivered until J.J. Hanbury had become Locomotive Superintendent, and he fitted them with large and rather ugly escape pipes leading from the top of the side tanks and meeting in a copper-capped orifice over the firebox; these did not improve the view ahead from the footplate. In the 'B' Class engines the back of the bunker was extended upwards to form a spectacle plate.

Between 1880 and 1885 17 of the 'A' and 'B' Class engines received new boilers, supplied by Beyer Peacock and fitted at the Metropolitan's Edgware Road workshops; these boilers were the same as the originals, and at the same time Adams bogies were substituted for the original Bissell trucks. In 1886 the Edgware Road workshops, which had restricted space, were abandoned in favour of the new works at Neasden which were much more commodious, and from then onwards most rebuilding of engines was done there. This included reboilering of 36 engines during the Hanbury regime, which entailed several modifications. Boiler pressure was increased to 150lbs and the dome, still with Salter spring-balance safety valves, was moved to the centre of the boiler barrel. Stovepipe chimneys were fitted, and two additional spring safety valves appeared over the firebox.

After T.F. Clark took over as Locomotive Superintendent in 1893, he introduced further modifications on rebuilt engines. Between 1894 and 1905 44 engines of Classes 'A' and 'B' were reboilered at Neasden. The spring-balance valves were removed from the domes and a pair of lock-up valves was placed over the firebox. The diameter of the coupled wheels was increased by one inch to 5ft 10in and cylinders were bored out to 17½in; boiler pressure was increased to 150lbs. Heating surface on the 'A' Class rebuilds was altered to 958.7sq ft, and on Class 'B' to 942.6sq ft. Cast iron bell-mouthed chimneys were introduced, though some engines retained the stovepipe pattern for some years. Several of the Clark rebuilds had the slide bars covered in, as a protection against dust.

By 1892 when the line had been extended to Aylesbury, some thought was given to providing the enginemen working over the open sections of the line with better protection from the elements than the existing weatherboards. Cabs had been disliked in earlier days by engine crews on the Inner Circle because they made their work very hot in the tunnels, but now they were running up to forty miles in the open air. Engine No.36 was fitted experimentally with a rudimentary cab by extending the weatherboard backwards over the footplate and supporting it with pillars. From 1895 enclosed cabs, which extended over the coal bunkers, were fitted to many locomotives, the first of these being Nos.3, 5, 10, 29 and 51. Some engines remained cabless until withdrawn, but all those which survived into the 1920s had received cabs.

One of the 1880-built series of *B Class* 4-4-0 tanks, Nos. 50-59, in original condition. Curved pipes from the safety valves to the top of the side tanks are to bring blow-off steam into the tanks, presumably to reduce its emission in the tunnels. Wooden brake blocks; sandbox on boiler behind dome; water filling point on top of tank behind weatherboard. The locomotive is in works grey.
Beyer Peacock & Co

Some trouble was experienced on the 4-4-0 tanks with coupling rods bending or breaking, no doubt due to the heavy stresses set up by constant starting and braking of trains at the frequent station stops on the Inner Circle. Bent rods were the cause of accidents at Sloane Square in 1873 and at Kings Cross in 1884, and Tomlinson began strengthening the coupling rods with iron. When Hanbury took over as Locomotive Superintendent in 1885 he started replacing the original rods with those of heavier section. The problem was finally solved when T.F. Clark replaced Hanbury in 1893; he fitted Gibson & Lilley link motion in place of the original Allan motion. This led to smoother running and also saved fuel, and by 1896 it had been fitted to all the Beyer tank engines, with consequent saving in wear and tear.

In 1898 No.62 was fitted experimentally with Holden's oil-burning apparatus, and two cylindrical oil tanks were placed on supports over the condenser pipes which ran along over the top of the side tanks. It was used on the Hammersmith to New Cross service, but no other engines were similarly treated at that time, as oil fuel of the right quality to prevent excessive smoke was too expensive. These oil tanks must have severely limited the enginemen's view of the track ahead. In 1921 'A' Class No.22 was similarly equipped for oil-burning, but this apparatus had been removed before it was sold to the District Railway in 1925.

In 1872 the Great Eastern Railway, which had opened several extensions in its suburban area, was short of locomotives, and it borrowed six 'A' Class engines, Nos.9, 10, 14, 15, 17 and 23, returning them five months later.

At the beginning of July 1878 the South Eastern Railway began a through service from Woolwich to Finsbury Park or Alexandra Palace on the Great Northern Railway, via the Metropolitan Widened Lines. Initially these trains were hauled by small Cudworth 0-4-4 well tanks, but these were underpowered for this work, and in April 1880 the SER arranged for three of the ten Metropolitan 4-4-0 tanks then under construction at Beyer Peacock to be delivered direct to the South Eastern; the SER paid £2,150 each for them, giving the Met a profit of £200 on each engine. They became South Eastern Nos.229, 300 and 301, being delivered at the end of May 1880. They performed very successfully on the through services to the GNR, but in June 1883 they were replaced by new South Eastern 'Q' Class 0-4-4Ts and transferred to Tonbridge shed. By the following August they were in store at Bricklayers Arms and on 7th November 1883 they were returned to the Metropolitan for the sum of £1,900 each, and received their Met running numbers, 57 to 59.

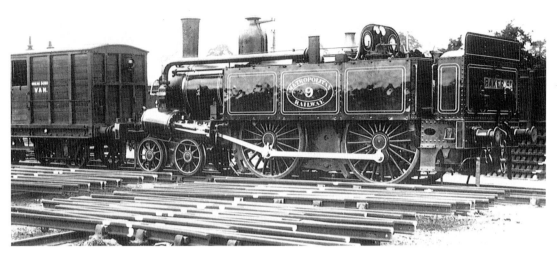

A *Class* 4-4-0T No.9, originally named 'Minerva', as rebuilt by Hanbury, with stovepipe chimney, dome on second ring of boiler and raised plate on back of bunker. Sandbox has been moved to below running plate; dark red livery with three-panel lining on side tanks.
Lens of Sutton

B *Class* 4-4-0T No.56, as rebuilt by T.F. Clark; the new boiler has a closed dome and lock-up safety valves on the firebox, but Hanbury's stovepipe chimney is still carried. The slide bars have been covered in as a protection against dust; the boiler pressure on these Clark rebuilds was increased by 20lbs to 150lbs. The location is probably Finchley Road and the date about 1900. Author's collection

The Beyer Peacock 4-4-0 tanks engines were a very successful design, and very similar locomotives were built for the District Railway (on which they were the standard and only design throughout the steam era), the Midland, the LNWR – a real tribute, because it was very rare for that company to purchase any engines not built at Crewe – the LSWR and the Rhenish Railway in Germany, making, with the 8 Tudela & Bilbao Railway machines, a total of 161 locomotives. On the Metropolitan they coped effectively with the Inner Circle traffic, with its frequent station stops, sharp curves, and gradients (stretches of 1 in 100 between Farringdon Street and Edgware Road, and about 1 in 70 from Kensington High Street to Notting Hill Gate).

A word is necessary here regarding the condensing apparatus. After an engine had been in service for some time with this apparatus working, the water in the tanks became too hot to be handled by the injectors, and therefore two pumps were fitted, driven by eccentrics on the driving axle. The tanks therefore had to be emptied periodically and refilled with cold water. Pipes were provided from the bottom of each tank, leading to a stop-valve under the footplate; when opened a tank-full could be discharged in just over a minute. Pits were provided at several stations to receive the hot water, originally at Bishop's Road and Farringdon Street and subsequently at Moorgate, Mansion House and Hammersmith. This emptying, with spectacular effects as engine and passengers on the platform disappeared in clouds of steam, was usually carried out where engines were changed, one engine coming off the train and being emptied and refilled, while another one took the train onwards. After some years the complete refilling with cold water was discontinued, which did not improve conditions in the tunnels.

District Railway 4-4-0T No.33, built by Beyer Peacock in 1881, as reboilered with closed dome, lock-up safety valves over the firebox, and cast chimney. Note Westinghouse brake; the sandbox is on the boiler behind the dome. The livery was dark olive green. No.33 survived, working ballast trains, until October 1925, when the District purchased Met A Class No.22 to replace it.
Author's collection

LSWR Met-type 4-4-0T No.323, built by Beyer Peacock in 1875, as fitted with an Adams stovepipe chimney. The handwheel for operating the Beattie patent feedwater heater is just in front of the side tank, near the sandbox, with a footstep for access to it. The six LSWR engines of this type never carried condensing gear; they only spent a short time in the London area, being employed for most of their lives on branches in the New Forest area. They were withdrawn from service between 1906 and 1913.
Author's collection

Until 1871 District Railway services between South Kensington and Blackfriars were worked by the Metropolitan, but in July of that year, coinciding with the District's extension from Blackfriars to Mansion House, the District acquired its own locomotives and coaching stock and operated its own train service. These locomotives were of the Beyer Peacock 4-4-0 type, similar to the Metropolitan engines. After the Inner Circle was completed in 1884, following much wrangling between the two companies, the Metropolitan worked all the trains on the outer rail (the clockwise direction) and a few trains on the inner (anti-clockwise) rail, leaving the District to operate the rest. This was presumably done to adjust for the different mileages of Circle route owned by the two companies. Changes of locomotives, when required, were made at South Kensington for trains on the outer rails, a process which sometimes took ten minutes. The Met engines were stabled at Edgware Road until the new engine sheds at Neasden were opened in 1884, and ran light to South Kensington for changing purposes; water was taken at Aldgate. Trains on the inner rail, Metropolitan and District, changed engines at Kensington High Street. Three Metropolitan engines, coupled together, used to arrive at Gloucester Road station from Edgware Road at about 5.45 am on Sundays to take up the 10-minute Circle service which began at about 6 o'clock. One of these engines ran forward to South Kensington, and the other two took out trains which were standing outside Gloucester Road.

The Metropolitan 'A' and 'B' Class 4-4-0 tanks worked over the whole of the Metropolitan system, including the Uxbridge branch from its opening on 4th July 1904 until it was electrified in January 1905. But until the Inner Circle was electrified in 1905 their chief task was hauling the trains on that line, as none of the later Metropolitan types of locomotive were used on the Circle. The Beyer tanks

A Class 4-4-0T No.24 of 1868 at Latimer Road, 30th March 1901, reboilered by Clark with cast-iron chimney, dome on middle ring, and lock-up safety valves; the weatherboard on the bunker was added by Hanbury. No.24 was sold to R. Fraser in 1913 and resold to Birtley Colliery nine years later.
LCGB Ken Nunn Collection

A Class 4-4-0T No.45 on a down train entering Rickmansworth station, circa 1900. It has been reboilered, with dome on the middle ring and cast chimney which carries the running number in brass numerals. Note the 'M.R.' lettering on the buffer-beam; Hanbury, the Met Locomotive Superintendent from 1885 to 1893, was previously at Derby and brought this practice with him. The first and third coaches are 'rigid-eights', which had side play in their axleboxes for negotiating curves, while the second vehicle is a four-wheeler; all are about thirty years old, and would have compared badly for comfort with the rolling stock used to serve the same stations by the Great Central on its recently-opened services from Marylebone. However, some improvement was being introduced by the Metropolitan at this time in the shape of the 'Ashbury' bogie stock. LCGB Ken Nunn Collection

A Class 4-4-0T No.17, originally named 'Ixion', on Chesham train at Harrow-on-the-Hill, 31st May 1902. Reboilered by T.F. Clark with polished, closed dome, lock-up safety valves on firebox, but still retaining stovepipe chimney. Engines rebuilt in this way, between 1894 and 1905, received 5ft 10in. diameter coupled wheels and cylinders bored out to 17¾in diameter; cast iron lipped chimneys were also usually fitted. This engine, together with Nos.9, 10, 14, 15 and 23, was lent to the Great Eastern Railway from July to November 1872 when that company was short of motive power on the Walthamstow, Chingford and Edmonton lines. LCGB Ken Nunn Collection

even put in an appearance on the Stanmore branch while it was being built in 1931-32, hauling contractors trains, and they may have performed a similar duty when the Watford branch was being constructed in 1925. When the Manchester, Sheffield & Lincolnshire Railway (later Great Central) was being extended to Marylebone, the 4-4-0 tanks were employed on trains of spoil removed from the tunnels in the St. John's Wood area, and handled 18 fully loaded wagons on St. John's Wood bank with ease.

When the line was extended to Harrow in 1880, a few of the Beyer Peacock tanks were stabled at that location, but when Neasden shed was opened a few years later they were transferred there. On the completion of the Inner Circle in 1884 most of the 4-4-0 tanks up to No.20 were at Neasden; Nos.27 to 33 were at New Cross for the East London line services, while those numbered between 21 and 50 were at Edgware Road. Nos.51 to 66 were stabled at Hammersmith for the Hammersmith & City line trains, which they shared with Great Western 2-4-0 tank engines. The Beyer engines also worked to Richmond, and were occasionally used on goods trains; they were very versatile engines, and certainly did all that was asked of them on many different duties.

Electrification was introduced from Baker Street to Harrow and Uxbridge on 1st January 1905 and on the Inner Circle on 24th September of that year, and this made many of the Beyer Peacock 4-4-0Ts redundant. E.L. Ahrons seemed to regret the passing of steam traction; he said that in the latter part of the 19th century the Met and District were really railways, 'but now, alas, they appear to be glorified overcrowded electric tramways. But today, the sulphur (from smoky locomotives) has all gone, except in the speech of a few irritated travellers, and has been replaced by an indescribable atmosphere of squashed microbes, and the sounds emitted by a hustler with a trumpet'. He conceded that this was purely a personal opinion, however, and it is unlikely that regular travellers on the Circle regretted the disappearance of the steam and sulphurous smoke which had filled the tunnels. Electrification, too, meant a considerable reduction in journey times.

A Class 4-4-0T No.33 at New Cross, 29th September 1900, as rebuilt by Hanbury in the late 1880s, with new boiler, dome on middle ring and stovepipe chimney. This engine was sold to R. Fraser of Newcastle-on-Tyne in 1907 for £235; its subsequent history is not known.
LCGB Ken Nunn Collection

Efforts were made to dispose of the surplus locomotives, and on 9th November 1905 an arrangement was made with Wheatley, Kirk, Price & Co, of 46 Watling Street, London, EC, to draw up a catalogue of all the engines which were for sale; a reserve price was put on each engine, and the firm were to submit to the Metropolitan any offers they received below those prices before effecting any sale. They would be allowed a commission of 5% on cash received from any sales effected. This arrangement is quoted in the minutes of the Metropolitan Stores Committee, who always handled the sale of the locomotives.

The majority of the 4-4-0 tanks were sold between 1906 and 1913 to R. Fraser & Sons, scrap merchants, of Newcastle-on-Tyne. Fraser had offered in 1906 to buy the entire stock of withdrawn engines at £220 each; he later increased this offer, and in the event he paid between £235 and £290 each for these engines, though Nos.51, 58, 59 and 65 realised only £160 each. Fraser resold several locomotives to various other railways and collieries, but the majority were cut up for scrap, some of them on site at Neasden. No.1, the first Beyer Peacock 4-4-0T, was withdrawn in 1897 after being damaged in an accident at Baker Street. By this time it had completed over a million miles, 632,000 miles of which were with its original boiler. It was then used as a stationary engine at Wembley Park to generate electricity for some experiments with the use of electric traction. No.7 had run 1,511,226 miles up to May 1908, though by then it was on its third boiler. Its career did not end then; it remained in service until 1925 when Fraser bought it and resold it to the Mersey Railway, where it replaced Met No.61, which the Mersey had purchased in 1907.

A full list of the disposal of the Beyer Peacock tank engines appears in Appendix III; the most interesting of the sales was that of Nos.10, 11, 12, 13, 15 and 66, sold to Cambrian Railways in 1905-7. These were renumbered as Cambrian Nos.2, 12, 33, 34, 36 and 37, and fitted with cabs. Their adhesion weight when the tanks were full, 33½ tons, however, was too much for the Cambrian underbridges and permanent way, so they were restricted to yard shunting and banking duties. In 1915 Cambrian

No.34 was converted into a 4-4-0 tender engine by Beyer Peacock; this reduced the weight on the coupled wheels to 27½ tons. No.36 was similarly treated in the following year, and these two engines were then able to work over the Moat Lane Junction and Brecon line. All six of the ex-Metropolitan engines passed into Great Western Railway ownership in 1922. The two 4-4-0 rebuilds were allocated GWR Nos.1113 and 1114, and the other four 4-4-0 tanks were allotted GWR Nos.1129 to 1132, but all six were withdrawn in 1922-23, so they probably never carried these new numbers.

Another engine which was rebuilt by its new owners was 'A' Class No.14, sold to the South Hetton Coal Co in 1905, where it became their No.6 and was converted to an 0-6-0 tank; it survived until 1948.

Of the 16 Metropolitan type 4-4-0 tanks purchased new by the London & North Western Railway in 1871-72, LNWR Nos.2055-2070, ten were rebuilt by Francis Webb as 4-4-2Ts in 1891-93, receiving new steel boilers and cabs in the process. But the most unusual rebuilding was that of No.2063 as a Webb 3-cylinder 4-2-2-0T in 1884. Later renumbered 1914 and then 3026, this locomotive was employed on the service between Mansion House and Willesden, and was withdrawn from service in 1897. Nos.2055 to 2070 were employed on suburban services from Euston and Broad Street, and also provided assistance up Camden Bank for many years. The five engines which remained in 4-4-0T form lasted until 1892-93, and the 4-4-2 tank rebuilds were withdrawn between 1907 and 1911.

In July 1868 the Midland Railway opened its line from Bedford to Kentish Town, and trains ran from there to Kings Cross junction and over the Met Widened Lines to Moorgate, as St Pancras station was not opened until the following October. The 2-4-0 tank engines built by Beyer Peacock for this service turned out, with their 16ft 6in wheelbase, to be unsuitable for the Metropolitan curves, so six of a batch of Metropolitan 4-4-0 tanks from Beyer Peacock were allocated to the Midland. They were MR Nos.204 to 209; they originally had condensing gear, and domes with Salter safety valves; the latter were retained when they received new Midland standard boilers in 1887-88. Additional lock-up safety valves were fitted on the fireboxes. They remained without cabs and worked in the London area until the turn of the century, when, fitted with cabs and with the condensing apparatus removed, they were transferred to the country area. They were withdrawn from service between 1906 and 1912.

Six engines of the Metropolitan type were purchased by the LSWR from Beyer Peacock in 1875. They did not receive condensing gear, but had cabs, closed domes on the first ring of the boilers, Ramsbottom safety valves over the fireboxes, cabs and Beattie's patent feedwater heaters. They were LSWR Nos.318 to 323, and were intended for fast passenger trains between Exeter and Plymouth, but they only spent a short time on these duties and were then transferred to the London area and used on the Leatherhead services. By the early 1900s most of them had gravitated to various branches in the New Forest area. William Adams removed the feedwater heaters and substituted stove-pipe chimneys for the original Beyer Peacock pattern, and No.318 acquired an Adams long-wheelbase bogie in place of its original Bissell truck. They were withdrawn between 1906 and 1913, No.320 being the last survivor of the class.

LNWR 4-4-2T No.3072 at Stockport, 16th May 1902. Sixteen Met-type Beyer Peacock 4-4-0 tanks were built for the North Western in 1871-72 and of these, ten were rebuilt by Francis Webb as 4-4-2T between 1891 and 1893, with new steel boilers and with cabs. These rebuilds were withdrawn between 1907 and 1911. LCGB Ken Nunn Collection

A fine view of *A Class* 4-4-0T No.26 in final condition, with cast iron chimney, condensing gear removed, later style of lettering, and crest on side of bunker. Built in 1868, this engine was sold, via R. Fraser, to Pelaw Main Colliery in 1926, where it survived until 1948. H. Gordon Tidey

The District Railway clung faithfully to the Met-type 4-4-0 tank design throughout the steam era, in fact the only other steam locomotives it ever possessed were two 0-6-0 tanks supplied by Hunslet in 1931. By 1886 they had acquired 54 of the Metropolitan type, Nos.1 to 54, and apart from reboilering, when cast chimneys and closed domes replaced the copper-capped chimneys and bell-mouthed domes with Salter safety valves originally fitted, they were largely unaltered by the time electrification made most of them redundant. At this time they were all without cabs; Nos.25-30, built in 1876, had cabs when delivered, but enginemen objected that these made work in the tunnels too hot, and they were removed. By 1909 all except Nos.33 and 34, retained for working ballast trains, had been withdrawn. No.33 was scrapped in 1925 and replaced by Metropolitan No.22; No.34, renumbered L34 and fitted with a cab, lasted until 1931.

To return to the Metropolitan Railway, the extension of electric traction to Rickmansworth in 1925 rendered more of the dwindling band of 4-4-0 tanks redundant, and in that year Nos.7, 22, 26, 42 and 44 were sold to R. Fraser, to be resold by him as shown in Appendix III. No.29 was broken up at Neasden in 1925, and three years later Nos.18 and 46 were purchased by A. Elvin, probably for scrap. So by the time London Transport absorbed the Metropolitan on 1st July 1933 only five, Nos.23, 27, 41, 48 and 49, remained in service.

Their declining years were spent on the Brill branch, and it is a happy thought that these veterans, like faithful workhorses put out to pasture, ended their lives in these sylvan surroundings. The Brill branch was opened in 1872, from Quainton Road, on the Aylesbury – Verney Junction line, to a station at Brill, quite a distance from the small village of that name. It had been built by the Duke of Buckingham and was entirely on his land, which meant that no Act of Parliament was necessary for its construction. Its title was the Oxford & Aylesbury Tramroad, but it got no nearer to Oxford than Brill, 6½ miles from Quainton Road. It was worked originally by two Aveling & Porter traction-engine-type locomotives, but when its working was taken over by the Metropolitan in 1899 it possessed two Manning Wardle 0-6-0 saddle tanks. After these were withdrawn, 'D' Class 2-4-0 tanks Nos.71 and 72 worked the branch, but these were sold in 1923 and 1916, and the only remaining engines with light enough axle-loading for the permanent way of the Brill line were the Beyer 4-4-0 tanks.

Far from the madding crowd. *A Class* 4-4-0T No.49 works out its closing years in sylvan surroundings on a Brill branch train near Wood Siding, 7th August 1933. LCGB Ken Nunn Collection

Two of these were allocated to this duty, and they worked on alternate weekly shifts, being kept in a small wooden engine shed at Brill. No.48 was on the branch prior to its withdrawal in 1936, but in the final years of the branch Nos.23 and 41 were the usual engines. Coaching stock consisted of 'rigid-eight' coaches dating from the early days of the Inner Circle, which had four wheels at each end, not in bogies but with sufficient side-play to allow them to negotiate curves. Like the engines which hauled them, it was a complete change of scene for these veterans; instead of being crowded with passengers on the Circle they were rarely filled as they meandered along the rural single-line byways of the Brill branch. At one time Locomotive No.41 could be seen coupled to coach No.41, a 'rigid-eight' which had been rebuilt at Neasden in a style similar to the 'Ashbury' coaches of 1898-1901.

But their days were numbered; road competition took away the sparse passenger traffic on the branch, which was closed on 30 November 1935. After this there was little use for the surviving 4-4-0 tank engines; No.27 was withdrawn in 1935; Nos.41, 48 and 49 shared the same fate a year later. No.23, however, renumbered L45 in 1937, remained in service until 1948, thus achieving an active life of 82 years. After withdrawal it was stored at Neasden, and it was restored there in 1960-61 to its 1903 condition. The cab was removed and a polished brass dome fitted; the livery is the Metropolitan dark red, with the side tanks lined in three equal-sized panels with 'Metropolitan Railway' in an oval scroll surrounding the number, 23, which also appears in brass numerals on the front of the chimney. Thus resplendent, it took part in the Underground Centenary celebrations in 1963, though not under its own power. Prior to this it had been on display at the Clapham Museum, later moving to the London Transport Collection at Syon Park. It is now on show at the London Transport Museum at Covent Garden.

It is very pleasing that a representative of this famous class of engines, which served Londoners so long and faithfully, has been preserved for posterity.

Two other experiments with 'A' Class locomotives should be mentioned. No.19 was used in connection with a device to solve the problem of the smoky atmosphere in the tunnel sections of the line, which was tested at Neasden in 1891-2. This was devised by Christopher Anderson and consisted of a rectangular tube between the rails, stretching for half a mile to a chimney at the 'exhausting station'. No.19 was fitted with a downward-pointing chimney which led into the tube by means of a 'slider'. This opened a series of valves to draw the smoke along the tube. The correspondent of the 'Willesden Chronicle' was impressed, but the device was never adopted.

In 1900 'A' Class No.1, which had been laid aside in 1897 after a runaway accident, was employed mounted on blocks, to generate current for an electrification experiment on the branch from Wembley Park to the Tower. This was carried out by Thomas Parker, proprietor of a Wolverhampton-based electrical engineering firm, and used a four-rail direct current system. Two 'Bogie' stock coaches were specially equipped with electric motors for the experiment, and the trials continued for about a year. At this time the joint Metropolitan/District Railway trials of electric working between High Street Kensington and Earls Court were also taking place, and the Met, evidently suspicious of the District Railway's influence, wanted to have its own evaluation of the feasibility of electric traction.

A Class 4-4-0T No.27 on an up ballast train near Harrow-on-the-Hill in August 1932. In their latter years the Beyer tanks were often used on this type of work and, as mentioned in the Introduction, my first sighting of one of these engines was on a ballast train at Amersham in the early thirties. Built by Beyer Peacock in 1867, No.27 was withdrawn by London Transport in 1935; it is shown in final condition and livery. NRM

Dimensions of Beyer Peacock 4-4-0 Tank Engines
All had 17in by 24in cylinders and coupled wheels 5ft 9in diameter.

Class 'A'			29-33 &	
Met No.	1-18	19-28	39-44	45-49
Boiler Pressure, lb/sq in	120	120	130	130
Total Heating surface, sq ft	1,014	1,014	1,014	1,014
Grate Area, sq. ft.	19	19	19	19
Weight, tons	42.15	42.6	42.6	42.3
Coal space, cu ft	44	67	67	54
Water capacity, gallons	1,000	1,000	1,000	1,000
Coupled Wheelbase	8ft 10in	8ft 10in	8ft 10 in	8ft 10in

Class 'B'	34-38 &	65-66
Met No.	50-64	
Boiler Pressure, lb/sq in	130	130
Total Heating Surface, sq ft	976	976
Grate Area, sq ft	18	18
Weight, tons	43.75	45.2
Coal Space, cu ft	56	56
Water Capacity, gallons	1,140	1,140
Coupled Wheelbase	8ft 1in	8ft 1in

Nos.1 to 33 and 39 to 49 had Bissell trucks when new.
Nos.34 to 38, and 50 to 66 had Adams bogies throughout.
The 'A' Class engines were fitted with Adams bogies when they came in for overhaul.

Prices of Beyer Peacock 4-4-0 Tanks

Met. Nos	Built	Price each	Met. Nos	Built	Price each	Met. Nos	Built	Price each
1 – 18	1864	£2,675	39 – 44	1869	£2,600	60 – 64	1884	?
19 – 23	1866	£2,675	45 – 49	1870	£2,545	65 – 66	1885	?
24 – 28	1868	£2,675	34 – 38	1879-80	£1,923			
29 – 33	1868-69	£2,675	50 – 59	1880	£1,950			

When built the first 18 engines had names, as follows:–

No.1 'Jupiter'	No.6 'Medusa'	No.11 'Latona'	No.16 'Achilles'
2 'Mars'	7 'Orion'	12 'Cyclops'	17 'Ixion'
3 'Juno'	8 'Pluto'	13 'Daphne'	18 'Hercules'
4 'Mercury'	9 'Minerva'	14 'Dido'	
5 'Apollo'	10 'Cerberus'	15 'Aurora'	

These nameplates were removed as the locomotives went through the shops for overhaul. The reason for this change in policy is not known; no more Metropolitan steam engines were named until the four 'G' Class 0-6-4Ts of 1915-16.

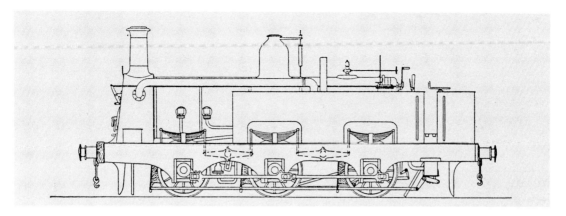

One of the five 0-6-0 Tank engines designed by R.H. Burnett for the Metropolitan & St Johns Wood Railway, and built by the Worcester Engine Co. in 1868. With 20″ × 24″ cylinders and coupled wheels 4ft in diameter, they were very powerful machines; in fact they were over-powerful for the St Johns Wood line, and they were sold in 1873-75, four to the Taff Vale Railway and one to the Sirhowy Valley Railway. *Railway Magazine*

3 The Burnett 0-6-0 Tanks

By 1864, with the original Bishop's Road to Farringdon Street section working successfully, the Metropolitan directors began to cast their eyes further afield. To the north west of Baker Street lay the Finchley Road district, a potential source of passenger traffic to the City, with the possibility of connections with the Midland Railway, whose London extension to St Pancras was then under construction, and with the LNWR's Hampstead Junction Railway. Junctions with these two lines could be expected to produce goods and passenger traffic over a Metropolitan extension from Baker Street. So the Metropolitan & St Johns Wood Railway was incorporated on 29th July 1864, as a semi-independent company, but one in which the Metropolitan had a large shareholding. This was to run from Baker Street to Swiss Cottage, with intermediate stations at St Johns Wood Road and Marlborough Road, and with an extension to Hampstead.

Opened as far as Swiss Cottage on 13th April 1868, the line involved some steep gradients, varying from 1 in 27 to 1 in 90. R.H. Burnett, the Met Locomotive Superintendent, considered that these would be too much for the Beyer Peacock 4-4-0 tanks, as the necessity of condensing in the tunnels would make it impossible to maintain full steam pressure for the whole length of the journey. He therefore brought out a design for a very heavy 0-6-0 tank engine, which would have plenty of power in reserve if steam pressure fell while the engines were condensing. Five of these locomotives, Metropolitan Nos.34 to 38, were delivered to this design by the Worcester Engine Co in 1868. With a working pressure of 130lbs per square inch, cylinders 20in by 24in, and coupled wheels 4ft in diameter, they were very powerful machines, and in fact their tractive effort at 85% boiler pressure was not exceeded on the Metropolitan until the 'K' Class 2-6-4 tanks came out in 1925.

It was soon discovered, however, that they were far more powerful than was necessary, and that the Beyer 4-4-0 tank engines could handle the trains of three 14 ton coaches without any difficulty. It was therefore decided to dispose of them, and a Board minute dated 4th November 1868 said that Myles Fenton, the General Manager, had approached the Midland Railway with a view to exchanging them for five of the Metropolitan type 4-4-0 tanks which were then being built for that company. Nothing came of this, however; the 0-6-0 tanks were probably too heavy and powerful for the Midland's needs. An offer received from the Monmouthshire Railway to purchase two of them, Nos.35 and 37, for £1,700 each, was declined, the Met asking £2,500 each, a price later reduced to £2,000. The Severn & Wye Railway "offered £1,500 for one of the company's spare engines", to quote the Met Stores Committee minute dated 1873, and this must refer to one of five 0-6-0 tanks, which had been withdrawn the previous year. But no sale was made to either of these companies, and eventually

Nos.34, 35, 37 and 38 were sold to the Taff Vale Railway, the first two in 1873 and the others two years later. They were given Taff Vale Nos.90, 91, 99 and 100. They were re-boilered while on the Taff Vale, and the condensing gear was removed. In their original condition they had Salter spring balanced safety-valves on the dome and copper capped chimneys, but on rebuilding they received closed domes with Ramsbottom safety-valves over the firebox; they were also fitted with cabs and chimneys of a different pattern.

These powerful outside-framed tank engines were very well suited for working the Taff Vale's heavy coal trains, and survived into the early years of the century, the last to be withdrawn being Taff Vale No.100, which was scrapped in October 1901, having been renumbered 276 two years previously.

Metropolitan No.36 had a very chequered career, and passed through several different owners. It was sold to the Sirhowy Valley Railway in 1873, and then passed by absorption to the LNWR in 1876, who renumbered it 2276, and then 1891 in 1877. In 1879 it was purchased by the Alexandra (Newport) Docks & Railway, where it became their No.5 and was named 'J.C. Parkinson'. It was later renumbered 26, and in 1920 it was sent to Hawthorn Leslie at Newcastle for conversion to an 0-6-2 tank. At the grouping it became GWR No.663 and survived until 1926, after being owned by no fewer than five different railway companies.

Dimensions were:

Cylinders	20in by 24in
Coupled wheels	4ft 0in diameter
Boiler Pressure	130lbs sq inch
Total heating surface	1,132 sq ft
Coupled wheelbase	14ft 0in
Grate area	22½ sq ft
Weight in working order	45 tons
Tractive effort at 85% pressure	22,100lbs

After rebuilding by the Taff Vale Railway, No.34, 35, 37 and 38 had their cylinders lined up to 17½in diameter, and the new boilers gave them an increased heating surface of 1,237.03sq ft, but the grate area was reduced to 15.83sq ft. Weight in working order was reduced by 11cwt.

Nos.34 to 38 were Worcester Engine Co Nos.35 to 39 in the same order, and cost £2,550 each.

Taff Vale Railway 0-6-0T No.91, formerly Met No.35, and one of five engines built in 1868 by the Worcester Engine Co. for the steeply graded St John's Wood extension. The Beyer 4-4-0 tanks were, however, quite capable of handling the traffic on this line, and four of the 0-6-0Ts, Nos.34, 35, 37 and 38, were sold to the Taff Vale Railway in 1873-75. This view shows the engine as rebuilt by the TVR with a cab and a new boiler. L&GRP

C Class 0-4-4T No.69 on a 2pm Liverpool Street to Verney Junction train near Pinner, 16th September 1911. This engine has been reboilered with closed dome, lock-up safety valves over the firebox, a cast-iron chimney and smokebox wingplates cut back. Condensing gear has been removed. The original boiler had a stovepipe chimney and Salter safety valves on the dome. Next to the engine is a four-wheeled brake van with cream waist and facia panels; apart from the Pullman car, which is in the original brown and cream livery (later superseded by all-over maroon), the remaining coaches are 'Ashbury' stock bogies, built at the turn of the century. LCGB Kenn Nunn Collection

4 C Class 0-4-4 Tank Engines

In 1892 the Metropolitan reached Aylesbury, which gave them a main line from Baker Street 38 miles long. Anticipating the need for additional locomotives to work this line, the Met broke away from the Beyer Peacock 4-4-0 tank design, the last of which had been delivered in 1885. John Bell, the General Manager, reported to the Board on 16 September 1891 that he had had an opportunity to purchase four 0-4-4 tank engines of James Stirling's SER 'Q' Class design from Neilson & Co at £2,200 each, and, relying on the approval of the Board (which was given) he had gone ahead and ordered them. Sir Edward Watkin was Chairman of the Metropolitan and of the South Eastern, and he was able to arrange for the use of 'Q' Class drawings in order to save time. Neilson had a batch of 'Q' Class engines in hand for the SER at the time, but the Metropolitan locomotives differed from these in having domed boilers with Salter safety valves instead of the Stirling domeless type, and there were also differences in some of the dimensions.

The use of the Stirling design may have saved time, but it certainly did not save money; it is interesting to note that the price of £2,200 each is £155 more than the SER paid for the similar engines built that year by Neilsons. The Metropolitan locomotives were designated 'C' Class and given running numbers 67 to 70; they were delivered in June 1891 and were put to work on the Chesham line services.

C Class 0-4-4T No.68, built by Neilson & Co, 1891, in final condition, with condensing apparatus and smokebox wingplates removed, and new boiler with closed dome and Ramsbottom safety valves on smokebox. A cast iron chimney has replaced the stovepipe originally fitted; the cab lookout has been partly enclosed and the bunker sides extended upwards to increase fuel capacity. Note tripcock apparatus between bogie wheels. No.68 was repainted in 1916 after a general overhaul at the Yorkshire Engine Co, and this was probably when it received the style of lettering shown here; previously the *C Class* had their running numbers in the centre of an oval scroll containing the words 'Metropolitan Railway'. This engine was sold in 1923 to Charles Williams of Morriston, Glamorgan, who later resold it to the Gwauncaegurwen Colliery. As can be clearly seen, the *C Class* were based on James Stirling's *Q Class* design for the South Eastern Railway. London Transport Museum

Dimensions were:–

Cylinders (inside)	17in by 26in	Grate area	15sq ft
Coupled Wheels	5ft 6in diameter	Total heating surface	921.5sq ft
Bogie wheels	3ft 9in diameter	Working pressure	140lbs per square inch
Wheelbase, total	22ft 0in	Tank capacity	1,050 gallons
Coupled Wheelbase	7ft 5in	Coal bunker capacity	59 cubic ft
Boiler	4ft 4in diameter, 10ft, 3½in long	Weight in working order	50 tons 8 cwt

They had stovepipe chimneys with a cast ring at the top; smokebox wingplates met the sandboxes on the leading coupled wheels. Condensing gear was fitted, large pipes leading from the smokeboxes into the top of the side tanks, which had vertical pipes near the cab to allow the escape of steam which failed to condense.

No.67 had an unfortunate start to its career. Working its first passenger duty on 4th June 1891, the 8.29am Rickmansworth train, it slipped badly and finally stuck altogether on the 1 in 60 gradient in the tunnel at Marlborough Road. The violent efforts of the engine, which was also blowing off strongly, caused the driver to lose consciousness, and the fireman, a locomotive foreman and a Neilson Reid fitter who were also on the footplate were semi-stupified. The signalman at St Johns Wood Road cabin had allowed the 8.34am train from Baker Street into the tunnel under the mistaken impression that he had received 'line clear' from Marlborough Road, and this, hauled by 'A' Class 4-4-0 tank No.17, ran into the rear of the stalled train. One coach was derailed and another lifted onto the front of No.17. Some injury resulted, though fortunately this was only slight, and the line was not cleared until 1pm.

The 'C' Class locomotives were employed chiefly on Aylesbury line trains, and it is doubtful whether they ever ventured onto the Inner Circle.

C Class 0-4-4T No.69 at Harrow, 31st May 1902, in original condition, with safety valves on dome and full smokebox wingplates. Built by Neilson & Co in 1891, this engine was rebuilt with a new boiler with closed dome and safety valves on the firebox in 1903. A cast chimney was then fitted and the smokebox wingplates were cut back. It was sold in 1923 to Charles Williams, a machinery merchant, of Morriston, South Wales. LCGB Ken Nunn Collection

No.70 received a new boiler of the original pattern, built at Neasden, in 1894, her first boiler therefore having a short life of only 3 years. Larger boilers were ordered from Hawthorn Leslie in September 1900, and fitted to No.67 in 1901, Nos.68 and 70 in 1902, and No.69 in 1903. These four boilers cost £605 each. The Salter safety valves were replaced by Ramsbottom valves over the firebox, and closed polished brass domes were substituted for the original open type. Dimensions were increased, to a total heating surface of 1,145.6sq ft and the grate area to 16.7sq ft. Working pressure was increased to 150lbs. Coal rails were added to the bunkers. The condensing gear was eventually removed and they received cast chimneys in place of the original stovepipe pattern, probably when further new boilers were fitted, which in the case of Nos.67 and 68 took place in 1915. At least one engine, No.68, received tripcock apparatus in its later days, and had its two coal rails on the bunker replaced by steel plates. Withdrawal was as shown in the table below.

Met No.	Built	Works No.	Disposal
67	1891	4352	Sold 1917 to Ministry of Munitions, Hereford National Filling Factory for £1,919.
68	1891	4353	Sold 1923 to Charles Williams, machinery merchant, Morriston, South Wales. Later resold to Gwauncae-gurwen Colliery Co Ltd.
69	1891	4354 ⎫	
70	1891	4355 ⎭	Sold 1923 to Charles Williams, Morriston.

'C' Class engines worked only on the open sections of the line; to Aylesbury (two were shedded there in 1892), Verney Junction – No.69 hauled the Liverpool Street to Verney Junction Pullman train in 1911 – and probably also on the Chesham branch. No.68 received a general repair at the Yorkshire Engine Co in 1915, and received the boiler from 'E' Class No.82 in 1920. No.69 had a new boiler in 1916, while No.70 received the boiler from 'E' Class No.79 one year later.

D Class 2-4-0T No.76, built by Sharp Stewart & Co. in 1895, at Neasden Shed, 2nd October 1920. The design was very similar to some engines which the same builder had supplied to the Barry Railway. Tripcock apparatus has been fitted behind the leading pony truck, and the original condensing gear has been removed. LCGB Ken Nunn Collection

5 **D Class 2-4-0 Tanks**

On 1st July 1891 the Metropolitan absorbed the Aylesbury & Buckingham Railway, which ran from Aylesbury to Verney Junction, worked since its opening in 1868 by the Great Western. Early in 1894 the latter declined to continue working this line, and the Met hired two locomotives from the LNWR. These were LNWR Nos.668 and 841; they arrived at Aylesbury on 30th March 1894, but three months later No.951 was substituted for No.668, which had broken a spring. These locomotives, which appear to have been Webb 2-4-0 engines, were hired for £2-10-0 each per day, and on 8th July 1894 one of them worked the Chalfont Road to Chesham shuttle service.

John Bell, the Metropolitan General Manager, told the Board in August 1894 that it was desirable that they should have their own motive power for the Aylesbury to Verney Junction line, and the company advertised through Davies & Co, of Cornhill, London, for suitable machines. As a result several engines were offered to them. These included an LNWR 2-4-0 tank which had belonged to the Duke of Sutherland and had worked at one of his collieries, offered at £300 by Markham & Co Ltd, of Chesterfield; two 2-4-0 tank engines from Beyer Peacock with 5ft 0½in coupled wheels and 15in by 20in cylinders, built in 1884 and 1885; 0-6-0 tanks by Vulcan Foundry at £1,300 and £1,750; by Kitsons at £1,650; by Neilsons at £1,400, and locomotives by Andrew Barclay and by Robert Stephenson. None of these options were taken up; the engines from Markhams were considered too small, and the Beyer Peacock machines would have needed expensive boiler repairs.

On 20th September 1894 two new 2-4-0 tank engines were ordered from Sharp, Stewart & Co. The design was credited to T.F. Clark, the Metropolitan's Locomotive Superintendent, but in fact they were very similar to some engines built by the same firm for the Barry Railway. They were to be delivered in 3½ months, and cost £1,575 each less 2½% discount. They bore Nos.71 and 72, and arrived at Aylesbury on 31st December 1894; they then went to Neasden for trials, taking up their duties on the Verney Junction line a month later, which brought an end to the hire of the LNWR locomotives. They had Ramsbottom safety valves over the firebox, bell-mouthed cast chimneys, and radial axleboxes for the leading wheels, with a side-play of 2¾in.

D Class 2-4-0T No.71, built by Sharp Stewart & Co in 1894, on a mixed train from Brill to Quainton Road, leaving Waddesdon, 24th June 1916. This engine was reboilered in 1911 and 1916, but its appearance was little altered; indeed, apart from the removal of condensing gear from Nos.73 to 76, the *D Class* were little changed throughout their lives, the new boilers they received being of the same pattern as the original ones. Nos.71 and 72 took over the Brill branch workings in the early 1900s after the two Manning Wardle 0-6-0 saddle tanks had been sold. Later these duties were taken over by *A Class* 4-4-0Ts.
LCGB Ken Nunn Collection

Dimensions were:–

Cylinders (inside)	17in by 24in	Total Heating Surface	1,091sq ft
Coupled Wheels	5ft 3in diameter	Tank capacity	800 gallons
Leading Wheels	3ft 6in diameter	Bunker capacity	1.8 tons
Coupled Wheelbase	7ft 9in	Weight in working order	41 tons 4cwt
Total Wheelbase	15ft 3in	Tractive effort	13,950lbs
Boiler Pressure	150lbs per square inch		

In May 1895 a further four locomotives were delivered by Sharp, Stewart. These, Nos.73 to 76, had slightly larger boilers with a grate area of 16¾sq ft as against 14½sq ft in Nos.71 and 72, a coupled and total wheelbase 3in longer, and weighed 2.3 tons more in working order. Nos.73 to 76 had Cartazzi leading axleboxes with a side-play of 1in, and were fitted with condensing apparatus, though it is difficult to see why, as they were prohibited from working through the tunnels between Finchley Road and Baker Street, and so could not work on the Inner Circle. A photograph of No.76 taken in 1920 shows it fitted with tripcock gear behind the leading wheels on the left hand side, and no doubt with similar equipment beneath the cab on the opposite side. The condensing apparatus was later removed; photographs show No.71 without it in 1916 and No.76 in 1920, but the 'D' Class seem to have been little altered otherwise during their rather short careers. They did, however, receive new boilers, the North British Locomotive Co supplying these in 1910 for Nos.71 and 72 at a cost of £555 each and for No.74 at £565. The following year Nos.73, 75 and 76 received new boilers from the Yorkshire Engine Co costing £499 each. When Nos.73 and 75 again required reboilering in 1917 Kerr Stuarts charged £1,090 each – a striking example of how wartime conditions caused inflated prices.

The 'D' Class engines do not seem to have been a great success; had Nos.73 to 76 been intended for goods work they would probably have had six coupled wheels. They worked passenger trains on the Aylesbury line, but their final years seem to have been spent mainly on goods trains, and in 1916 No.71 was at work on the Brill branch. They were withdrawn as shown in the table below.

Met. No.	Built	Works No.	Disposal
71	1894	4055	Sold to Charles Williams, Morriston, Glamorgan, 1923.
72	1894	4056	Sold to Ministry of Munitions, 1916 for £1,450.
73	1895	4075	Sold to Charles Williams 1923.
74	1895	4076	Sold to Charles Williams, 1923; later resold to United National Collieries, Nine Mile Point Colliery, Mon.
75	1895	4077	Sold to Charles Williams 1923; later resold to Baldwins Ltd., Port Talbot; scrapped as their Nº6 in 1930.
76	1895	4078	Sold to Charles Williams, 1923.

Williams paid only £220 each for Nos.71 and 73 to 76, much less than the Government had paid for No.72 seven years earlier, so he would appear to have had a bargain.

No. 71 received a new boiler in 1911, and a general repair at the Yorkshire Engine Co. five years later. Nos.72, 73 and 74 were fitted with new boilers between 1911 and 1916; no.75 received an "E" Class boiler in 1909, and no.76 had its cylinders bored out to 17½" diameter in 1914.

E Class 0-4-4 tank No.77, built at Neasden in 1896 at a cost of £2,080 15s 7d, in the elaborately-lined livery in which this class was originally finished, and with cast number-plate. The original Met coat of arms appears on the sandbox; this consisted of two tunnel-mouths, with a train approaching in the left-hand track and another train receding on the right-hand pair of metals. These were surmounted by the arms of the City of London, and the whole design was surrounded by elaborate scrollwork. No.77 was renumbered L46 by London Transport, and withdrawn in 1962. Lens of Sutton

6 **E Class 0-4-4 Tanks**

By 1896 increased Extension Line traffic created a need for more locomotive power, and early in that year the Stores Committee ordered various components for two 0-4-4 tank engines, to be built at Neasden. These, designed by T.F. Clark, were an enlargement of the Stirling-type 'C' Class machines, and became Nos.77 and 78, costing £2,080-15-7 each, and entering traffic in 1896. A third engine, completed at Neasden two years later, became No.1, taking the number of the first Beyer Peacock 4-4-0 tank, which had been damaged in an accident in 1897 and withdrawn. In October 1898 Clark recommended that a further two locomotives should be built at Neasden at a cost of about £1,813 each; this was approved by the directors but not carried out, and instead tenders were invited for the manufacture of four more engines. Six firms quoted for these and, unusually, it was the most expensive tender, from Hawthorn Leslie & Co at £3,392 each, which was accepted on 28th March 1900, with delivery in eight months. Two engines, Nos.79 and 80, were delivered at the end of the year, while Nos.81 and 82 followed in April 1901. Cylinders in the Hawthorn Leslie locomotives were ½ inch larger in diameter than those in the Neasden-built machines, dimensions being as follows:–

Cylinders (inside) Nos.1, 77 & 78	17in by 26in	Heating surface, boiler	1,050sq ft
		Heating surface, firebox	95.6sq ft
Nos.79-82	17½in by 26in	Total	1,145.6sq ft
Coupled wheels	5ft 6in diameter	Working pressure	150lbs sq inch
Bogie wheels	3ft 9½in diameter	Tank capacity	1,200 gallons
Coupled wheelbase	7ft 5in	Bunker capacity	87.8 cubic ft
Total wheelbase	22ft 1in	Weight in working order	54 tons 10cwt
Grate area	16.7sq ft		

E Class 0-4-4T No.78 at Chesham in March 1931 on the branch train. Condensing gear has been removed and the bunker capacity increased by the addition of steel plates in place of the original small coal rails. Two 'Dreadnought' coaches, as shown, was the normal make-up of the Chesham branch train. Dr Ian C. Allen

Classified 'E', they had closed domes on the middle ring of the boiler, cast bell-mouthed chimneys, and sandboxes on the leading coupled-wheel splashers. When delivered, condensing gear was fitted, pipes from the smokebox leading to the top of the side tanks, which also had small vertical pipes in front of the cab to allow uncondensed steam to escape, but the condensing apparatus was removed after a few years, probably because after electrification to Harrow-on-the-Hill in 1905 the 'E' Class rarely penetrated the tunnel sections of the railway. Originally the bunkers had two coal rails, but these were later replaced by taller steel plates to increase the coal capacity. Photographs of Nos.1 and 82, probably taken in the 1920s, show them with Westinghouse brake pumps in front of the side tanks and cylindrical reservoirs on top of the tanks, but these were later removed. Tripcock apparatus was also fitted to the 'E' Class engines.

'E' Class engines worked the majority of the Aylesbury line services beyond Harrow-on-the-Hill until the appearance of the 'G' Class 0-6-4 tanks in 1915/16, and still occasionally appeared on these workings afterwards; though after the 'H' Class 4-4-4Ts were delivered such duties for the 'E' Class were rarer. However, they were kept in reserve and sometimes took over Aylesbury trains when locomotive power was in short supply, even after the LNER took over responsibility for steam Metropolitan services in 1937. One would usually stand by in the Watford line bay at Rickmansworth, and would often be pressed into service on Aylesbury trains, especially in the years after World War II, when low standards of maintenance at Neasden LNER shed created a shortage of serviceable engines. The Chesham branch was a regular haunt of the 'E' Class right up to 1938.

However, three of them were withdrawn in 1935, and No.80, now renumbered L47 was withdrawn in 1941.

E Class 0-4-4T No.80 at Neasden, 17th May 1924. Built by Hawthorn, Leslie & Co in 1900, it is shown in final condition with condensing gear removed. It received new boilers in 1914 and 1923; note tripcock apparatus between bogie wheels. No.80 received its last general repair at Neasden in March 1937 and was renumbered L47 by London Transport, being withdrawn from service four years later. The brass numerals have been removed from the chimney, and the running number on the side tanks is larger than before. LCGB Ken Nunn Collection

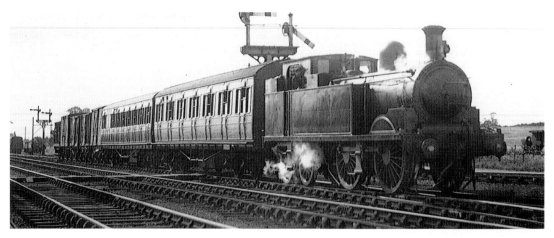

Above *E Class* 0-4-4T No.1 on a mixed train from Chesham arriving at Chalfont, 17th June 1933. The two 'Dreadnought' coaches are a first class coach next to the engine with a brake third following. The *E Class* were regular performers on Chesham branch trains, which used a bay platform on the up side of Chalfont station.
LCGB Ken Nunn Collection

E Class 0-4-4T No.1 on Chesham branch train consisting of two 'Dreadnought' coaches, leaving Chalfont, 17th June 1933. LCGB Ken Nunn Collection

London Transport numbers were allocated in 1937 to the four survivors, and withdrawal of the class was as shown in the table.

Met. No.	Builder	Date	Works No.	LPTB No.	Withdrawn
1	Neasden	1898	-	L44	1963
77	Neasden	1896	-	L46	1962
78	Neasden	1896	-	-	1935
79	Hawthorn, Leslie	1900	2474	-	1935 (sold)
80	Hawthorn, Leslie	1900	2475	L47	1941
81	Hawthorn, Leslie	1901	2476	L48	1963
82	Hawthorn, Leslie	1901	2477	-	1935 (sold)

It was evidently intended at one time to build further 'E' Class engines, as running numbers 83 to 89 were never used, but impending electrification eventually made this unnecessary.

Happily, No.1 (LPTB No.L44) has been preserved. After withdrawal it was sold to the London Railway Preservation Society, and after storage at two locations in Bedfordshire it ended up at Quainton Road, headquarters of the Quainton Railway Society, back on Metropolitan territory. Owing to other commitments, restoration has been a long process, but in 1987 L44 emerged in working order, resplendent in Metropolitan Railway livery and with its original running number, 1.

In the late 1950s, when the 'E' and 'F' Class engines were growing old and maintenance costs were rising, London Transport contemplated renewing them with boilers from ex-South Eastern & Chatham Wainwright 'H' Class 0-4-4 tank engines. But this was never done. LT experimented with a BR 350hp diesel-electric shunter and with 'J52' Class 0-6-0ST No.68852, but neither of these was suitable and, in the event, it was decided to purchase Western Region '57xx' 0-6-0 pannier tanks to replace the ageing Metropolitan locomotives.

L44 was involved in hauling several enthusiasts' special trains; on 4th July 1954 it worked a special over the Uxbridge branch, to mark the fiftieth anniversary of the time when, as Met No.1, it had hauled the branch's opening train. Three years later it hauled a special round the Inner Circle. Finally, on October 1st 1961, it appeared at the head of a Southern Counties Touring Society train which visited New Cross Gate on the East London Line, probably the first time an 'E' Class engine had been there.

It is interesting to note that the Hawthorn Leslie engines cost considerably more, at £3,393 each, than Nos.77 and 78 which were built at Neasden for only £2,080-15-7 each; presumably Neasden works was too busy to construct the further four engines required, which had to be put out to Hawthorn Leslie instead.

In 1914, Nos.77 and 82 were fitted with Westinghouse brakes, centre buffers and automatic couplers, presumably for shunting and marshalling electric coaching stock. The whole class received new boilers; Nos.1, 77 and 78 in 1909 (these boilers were supplied by the Yorkshire Engine Co at £1,483-10-0 for the three); No.79 in 1917, No.80 in 1914 and 1923, No.81 in 1923, and No.82 in 1917. The new boilers fitted in 1923 were made by Kerr, Stuart & Co, and cost £1,405-12-7 each, only slightly less than all three of those supplied by Yorkshire Engine Co in 1909.

On 16th January 1902 a special train conveyed King Edward VII from Baker Street to Amersham; he was going to Penn as a guest of Lord Howe. In his report to the Board A.C. Ellis, the Met General Manager, stated that the train left Baker Street a few minutes late at 6.16pm, owing to the King's party being a few minutes late in joining the train; it covered the 24 miles to Amersham with an unobstructed run in 36 minutes. On arrival at Amersham the King expressed his satisfaction with the arrangements. Tantalisingly, Ellis's report gives no details of the rolling stock used on this, probably the only Royal Train ever run over the Metropolitan, but it seems reasonable to suppose that the locomotive used would have been one of the 'E' Class, at that time the most modern passenger engines possessed by the company. King Edward and his entourage would almost certainly have been conveyed in the two six-wheeled saloons built for the use of Lord Rothschild by Brown Marshalls in 1895 (these were rebuilt as a single bogie saloon at Neasden in 1905) and the rest of the train would probably have been 'Bogie' stock coaches.

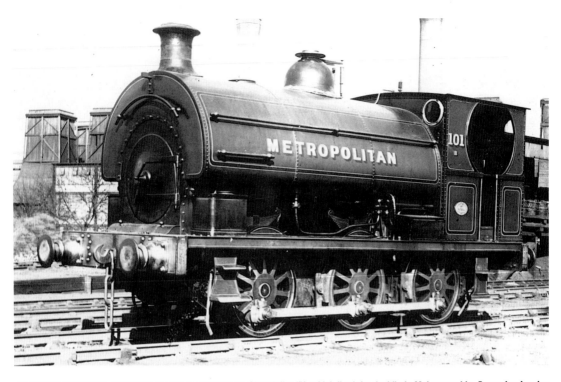

Peckett 0-6-0ST No.101, built 1897. It carries, erroneously, Class letter 'B', which it retained while in Met ownership. Becoming London Transport L53 in 1937, it was scrapped in 1960; for most, and probably all of its life, it remained at Neasden. The power station can be seen in the background, and on right part of the coaling stage is visible. Loco Publishing Co

7 Peckett 0-6-0 Saddle Tanks

In March 1897 an 0-6-0 saddle tank was delivered by Pecketts of Bristol; this was of their standard 619 class design, and cost £1,390, becoming Metropolitan No.101. A similar engine, No.102, was ordered in November 1899 at a cost of £1,595. These were for shunting at Neasden and Harrow, and dimensions were as follows:–

Cylinders (inside)	16in by 22in	Grate area	13.25sq ft
Coupled wheels	3ft 10in diameter	Working pressure	140lbs sq inch
Wheelbase	11ft 0in	Tank capacity	1,160 gallons
Boiler barrel	8ft 6in long, 3ft 10in diameter	Bunker	45.6 cubic ft
Total heating surface	712sq ft	Weight in working order	39 tons

Soon after delivery No.101 was pressed into service hauling spoil trains over the Metropolitan line during the construction of the Great Central Railway approach to Marylebone, before the Lord's Ground tunnel was finished. Both engines remained virtually unaltered throughout their life; No.102 received new cylinders in 1906. They do not appear to have received a class letter, but a photograph of No.101 shows it with 'B' underneath its running number; this was presumably an error. They were of a very neat appearance, with flared chimneys, Salter safety valves on the domes and rectangular sandboxes on the footplate, in front of the leading wheels. During their latter years in London Transport ownership No.101, renumbered L53, remained at Neasden, while No.102, now L54, was at Lillie Bridge depot. Their works numbers were 664 and 823, and they were withdrawn in 1960 and 1961 respectively.

Peckett 0-6-0ST No.102 at Neasden in 1924 where it had been in store since the previous year. Of the maker's standard design, it was ordered in November 1899 at a cost of £1,595. After a period of loan to the District Railway in 1925, its times spent in traffic were sporadic, as the Met and LNER were responsible for shunting at Harrow only in alternate five year periods. No.102 received a Jones patent blastpipe in 1920, and a general overhaul in May 1935. During its later London Transport years it was usually at Lillie Bridge, performing the duties for which the District had hired it in 1925. It was withdrawn as LT No.L54 in 1961. Photomatic

In 1925 No.102 was on hire to the District Railway, to replace District No.33, a Metropolitan-type 4-4-0 tank, which they were about to withdraw. The District's other surviving 4-4-0 tank, No.34, was at this time under repair at Neasden. In February 1925 the District asked the Metropolitan if they could purchase Nos.101 and 102, or two more Metropolitan 4-4-0T engines. The Met decided they wanted to retain both the Peckett 0-6-0 tanks, and the upshot was that the District purchased Metropolitan No.22 in April 1925 for £300. This became District No.35 and lasted until 1931.

No.101 received general repairs in 1911 and 1921, receiving a new copper firebox and new cylinders on the latter date; its last general repair while in Metropolitan ownership was on 6th April 1933. No.102 had general repairs in 1923; it had been fitted with a Jones patent blast pipe years earlier.

Neither of the Peckett saddle tanks required new boilers, as their chief duty was that of shunting at Harrow goods yard; this yard was jointly owned by the Metropolitan and the Great Central (later LNER), and under the terms of the Met & GC Joint Committee agreement the two companies shared this shunting duty in alternate five-year periods. Consequently the tasks of the Peckett 0-6-0STs were never very arduous, and they spent some of their time in store. They did occasionally venture out onto the main line, however, and one of their duties was that of hauling the daily Neasden to Willesden Green goods train.

In 1893 a siding had been constructed from Wembley Park station into the Park, to convey materials used in building Sir Edward Watkin's ill-fated Tower. This siding was utilised in 1906 to remove the remains of the dismantled Tower, but it was taken up in 1909, and it is very probable that one of the Peckett 0-6-0STs was used for this operation.

When No.102 was first repainted in London Transport livery prior to 1936, the Metropolitan dark red colour was applied without lining out, but both engines were later fully lined out.

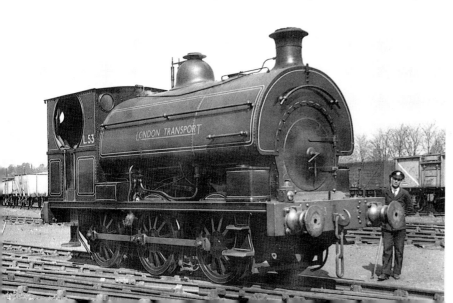

Peckett 0-6-0ST L53 (Met No.101), built 1897 and withdrawn from service in 1960. This and its sister engine, Met No.102, were supplied for shunting at Neasden and Harrow. No.101 received a new copper firebox and new cylinders in 1921, but neither engine was much altered during its career. This view shows it at the Power Station sidings at Neasden on 13th April 1957. Author

F Class 0-6-2T No.92 shunting at Aylesbury, 24th June 1916. Built in 1901 by the Yorkshire Engine Co, this engine became London Transport No.L51 in 1937 and was withdrawn twenty years later. Note the running number in small numerals on the side tank — an unusual feature for this class. KCGB Ken Nunn Collection

8 F Class 0-6-2 Tanks

By 1900 goods traffic on the Aylesbury line was growing, and the Metropolitan did not possess any locomotives really suitable for handling it. So tenders were invited from five builders for four 0-6-2 tank engines, to the design of T.F. Clark, the Met Locomotive Superintendent. The prices quoted were as follows;–

Sharp, Stewart & Co	£3,290 each
Yorkshire Engine Co	£3,350 each
Dubs & Co	£3,300 each
Neilson, Reid & Co	£3,375 each
Robert Stephenson & Co	£3,300 each

The Yorkshire Engine Company's tender was accepted on 23rd May 1900, one engine to be delivered within six months and the other three by the end of the year. In the event, however, all four were delivered in May 1901. Apart from their wheel formula they were very similar to the 'E' Class 0-4-4 tanks which Clark had designed a few years earlier. They had cast bell-mouthed chimneys, Ramsbottom safety-valves over the firebox, and condensing gear, though this was soon removed. Just why it was ever fitted is rather a puzzle, as goods traffic hauled by Met steam locomotives did not penetrate the tunnels south of Finchley Road. Smokebox wingplates joined the sandboxes on the leading coupled-wheel splashers, which had brass beading. Being intended purely for goods traffic, they did not receive steam train heating apparatus.

F Class 0-6-2T No.92 at Neasden, circa 1930. Part of the engine shed can be seen in the right background.

Dimensions were as follows:–

Cylinders (inside)	17½in by 26in	Coupled Wheelbase	16ft 0in
Boiler Pressure	150lbs sq inch	Grate area	18sq ft
Total Heating Surface	1,150sq ft	Water capacity	1,430 gallons
Weight in working order	56 tons	Coal Capacity	2½ tons
Coupled wheels	5ft 2in diameter	Tractive Effort (85%)	16,350lbs

They were the last steam locomotives built to the loading gauge of the line south of Finchley Road, and also the last turned out in the old style with 'Metropolitan Railway' in a double oval on the side tanks, and brass chimney numerals and 'M.R.' on the bufferbeams.

As noted above, they were intended for freight train duties, and I know of no recorded instances of their use on passenger traffic. They were the mainstay of freight motive power until the 'G' Class 0-6-4 tanks arrived in 1915-16, though 'D' Class Sharp Stewart 2-4-0Ts were occasionally seen hauling goods trains. The Harrow & Stanmore Gas Co. had a siding, opened in 1910, at South Harrow to serve their gasworks, and 'F' Class engines were used on a daily coal train from Neasden to these sidings. The 1927 working timetable says that this train could be propelled between Gas Works Siding and Rayners Lane provided the load did not exceed 20 vehicles; this was probably because the siding was single track and without engine run-round facilities. Besides freight train haulage to Verney Junction, Uxbridge, Stanmore and Rickmansworth, the 'F' Class were employed on shunting work and worked engineering trains, including those on the Hammersmith & City line. Their use in freight service would, after the coming of the 'G' Class 0-6-4Ts and 'K' Class 2-6-4Ts, be confined to lighter trains; one of these was an occasional goods train which worked from Neasden (Met) goods yard to Willesden Green or Uxbridge. One of the Peckett 0-6-0 saddle tanks was also sometimes used on this duty. During the Harrow quadrupling and the construction of the Stanmore branch in 1930-32 'F' Class locomotives were used on these works. Another duty was the hauling of trains containing dirty ballast from track renewals to Watford Tip Sidings.

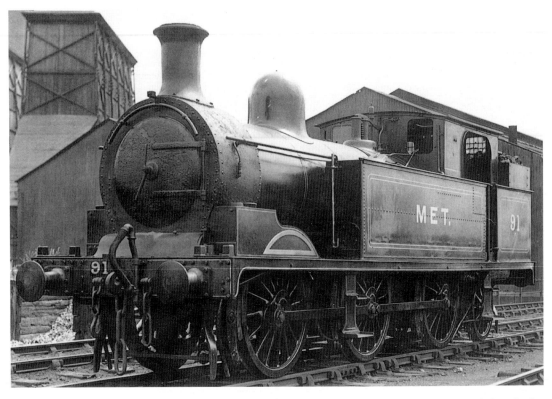

F Class 0-6-2T No.91 at Neasden, 11th July 1936. This was built by the Yorkshire Engine Co in 1901. It originally carried condensing gear, but apart from the removal of this it was very little altered throughout its existence. It became No.L50 under the London Transport renumbering scheme, and survived until 1958. It received a general overhaul at Neasden in March 1934, when the 'MET' lettering was applied. The LPTB did not decide on the 'London Transport' fleet name until 1934, and this 'MET' style was presumably used as an interim measure. At the same time, the number 91 was painted on the buffer beam. H.C. Casserley

Nos.90, 91 and 92 received new boilers supplied by Kerr Stuart & Co between 1917 and 1919, and No.93 received a heavy repair at that company's works at Stoke-on-Trent in 1918, when it was fitted with a new boiler made by the Yorkshire Engine Co. The smokebox wingplates were removed when the new boilers were fitted. At least two engines, Nos.90 and 93, received Westinghouse brakes, with a cylindrical reservoir on top of the left hand side tank and the pump immediately in front of the tank. These were apparently fitted after 1937, as Neasden works records prior to that date make no mention of them. Like the 'E' Class 0-4-4 tanks, 'F' Class engines had the coal rails on their bunkers replaced by extended metal plates to increase capacity. Tripcock apparatus was fitted to Met engines which worked over electrified lines, and this was carried out with the 'F' Class in about 1925 at a cost of £22 per engine; the tripcock was fitted behind the leading coupled wheels on the right hand side and in front of the pony truck wheels on the opposite side.

By the late 1950s the 'E' and 'F' Class engines were ageing and becoming beyond economic overhaul. Consideration was given to reboilering them with ex-South Eastern & Chatham 'H' Class 0-4-4T boilers, but nothing came of this. Diesel locomotives were too expensive for the limited work they would be called upon to do, though a BR 350hp diesel electric shunter, No.13018, was tried out. Western Region 0-6-0 pannier tank No.7711 was purchased by London Transport in 1956, becoming No.L90, and was most successful; it was followed by 11 other pannier tanks which by 1963 had replaced the Met 'E', 'F' and Peckett 0-6-0ST classes. Withdrawal dates of the 'F' Class were as follows:–

Met No.	Works No.	L.T. No.	Withdrawn
90	624	L49	1957
91	625	L50	1958
92	626	L51	1957
93	627	L52	1962

After withdrawal L52 was retained to take part in the Underground centenary celebrations, and the London Railway Preservation Society made an attempt to purchase it for preservation. In the event they acquired 'E' Class L44 instead, and L52 was cut up outside the Neasden shed, together with 'E' Class L48, in July 1964. These had been the last survivors, in regular service, of a long line of Metropolitan Railway steam locomotives.

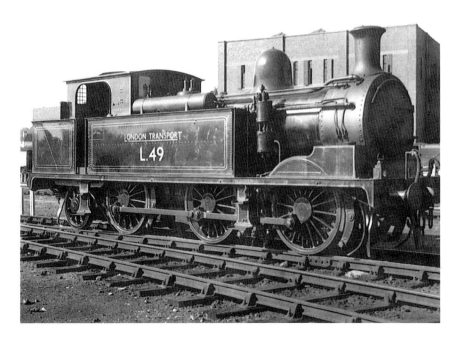

Above *F Class* **0-6-2T L52 (Met No.93) on a breakdown train from Neasden arriving at Farringdon, 23rd May 1954.**
LCGB Ken Nunn Collection

F Class **0-6-2T L49 (Met No.90), fitted with Westinghouse brakes and tripcock gear, shining in the sun at Neasden, 1st September 1953. A new boiler from Kerr Stuart was fitted in 1919, and it was one of the last engines overhauled at Neasden Works, receiving a general repair there in October 1937, only a month before the loco works closed on the transfer of the larger Met locomotives to the LNER.** Author

G Class 0-6-4T No.94 'Lord Aberconway' in photographic grey livery. The first of a class of four engines, No.94 was built by the Yorkshire Engine Co at a price of £3,621 and delivered to Neasden on 30th November 1915. The lettering is the original style and the brass number plate has been painted for photographic purposes. Sliding shutters to the cabside openings, and tripcock apparatus have not yet been fitted. Lord Aberconway, formerly Sir Charles B.B. McLaren, was Chairman of the Metropolitan from 1904 until 1933. The *G Class* engines experienced trouble with cracked frames on several occasions, probably due to the six-coupled wheelbase when negotiating yard curves. No.94 suffered in this way in 1928, receiving new frames, boiler and cylinders at Kerr Stuarts. Into traffic again on 11th October 1928, a connecting rod broke six weeks later and smashed the front of the cylinders. So a further pair of cylinders from Kerr Stuart were fitted at Neasden, the engine finally being back at work on 19th June 1929. After transfer to the LNER in November 1937, No.94 became Class 'M2' No.6154; allocated 1946 scheme number 9075, it was scrapped in May 1947 before carrying it. London Transport Museum

9 **G Class 0-6-4 Tanks**

In December 1910 Robert H. Selbie, the Metropolitan General Manager, had recommended to the Board that four higher capacity locomotives should be obtained, mainly to deal more economically with goods traffic. At this time the only goods engines the company owned were the four small 0-6-2 tanks of Class 'F', and these could not handle the weight of the goods trains without a disproportionate coal consumption. The new passenger stock was also heavier than the older coaches, so difficulty was also experienced with passenger trains. This matter came up again at the Board meeting on 27th June 1912, when it was resolved that tenders for the supply of these four locomotives should be obtained. But in May 1913 Selbie said that tenders received had exceedingly heavy prices, and so he would negotiate with other railway companies to see if suitable engines could be obtained secondhand.

But in a further report to the Board on 17th September 1914 Selbie said he had not been able to do so, and he recommended that the new engines should be ordered; they were to replace obsolete and inefficient types. They were mainly for passenger work and should be able to haul a maximum of eight coaches, weighing about 250 tons, have good acceleration and be capable of high speed between stations. They should also be capable of handling 40 coal wagons, or 55 goods wagons, together with a brake van, making a total weight of 650 tons. The maximum gradient on the line was 1 in 90. They should not exceed 70 tons in weight, and should have Robinson superheaters, automatic, steam and hand brakes, and steam sanding.

G Class 0-6-4T No.97 'Brill' on an up passenger train at Aylesbury, circa 1930. When introduced in 1915, the *G Class* were intended for freight traffic, which had increased considerably during the Great War. With 5ft 9ins diameter coupled wheels, however, they were really mixed traffic engines and, as shown here, were occasionally used on passenger services. When negotiating curves in sidings, they were prone to cracking of the frames, and in June 1928 Nos.96 and 97 were both out of action for this reason. No.97 was delivered from the Yorkshire Engine Co. on March 18th 1916 at a cost of £3,956; it received the boiler from *H Class* 4-4-4T No.106 six years later, and a new boiler during overhaul at Kerr Stuart & Co's Stoke-on-Trent works in 1929. In 1934 it received the boiler from its sister, No.96. Becoming *LNER M2 Class* No.6157, it was first of the class to be withdrawn, in January 1943.

The matter of wheel formula was left open. Tenders were received from six builders, as follows:-

Yorkshire Engine Co	£3,600 each
Kitson & Co	£3,730
Robert Stephenson & Co	£3,771
Beyer Peacock & Co	£3,850
Hawthorn, Leslie & Co	£3,970
North British Locomotive Co	£4,950

The Yorkshire Engine Co's design, for a 0-6-4 tank engine, was the one which was accepted. Full details of the schemes put forward by the other manufacturers are missing, but it is understood that North British produced two 0-8-4 tank engine designs. These would have been more powerful than the Metropolitan required, too heavy and too expensive. Beyer Peacock proposed a four-cylinder 4-6-4 tank developed from the Dutch State Railways 4-6-0 design which had been built by Beyer Peacock in 1910. This proposal, weighing 95½ tons, was well over the maximum stipulated in the Met's specification, and so was a non-starter.

Selbie told the Board 'The engine the Yorkshire Engine Co propose to supply appears to be equal to the others and to satisfy our requirements'. It had the additional virtue of being the cheapest option, and so this was the tender which was accepted. Two engines were ordered on 17th September 1914, at £3,600 each, delivery to be made in 9 months. On 28th January 1915 the Met Board approved the ordering of two further engines, but Selbie was unable to obtain these two at the same price; they would cost £3,935, a considerable increase in the space of only five months, though wartime conditions may have been to blame for this.

So the design of these four 0-6-4 tank engines, usually attributed to Charles Jones, the Metropolitan Chief Mechanical Engineer, was really left to the Yorkshire Engine Co, Jones having given merely a broad specification. This is confirmed by the fact that in the report to the Met Board, quoted above, Selbie said 'I have recently obtained prices from 6 firms and asked them to submit their own designs for two locomotives to comply with the above requirements'.

The new locomotives, classified 'G', were delivered as follows, and the prices were slightly higher than those originally quoted, i.e.

Met No.	Works No.	Delivered	Cost
94	1283	30/11/15	£3,621
95	1284	30/12/15	£3,621
96	1301	2/2/16	£3,956
97	1302	18/3/16	£3,956

They had the following dimensions:–

Cylinders (2 inside)	20in by 26in	Grate area	21.4sq ft
(Stephenson valve motion		Boiler Pressure	160lbs sq in
with piston valves)		Coupled wheels	5ft 9in diameter
Heating surface		Trailing wheels	3ft 6in diameter
Firebox	132sq ft	Tractive Effort (85%)	20,498lbs
Tubes (143 by 1¾in)	744sq ft	Length over buffers	41ft 2in
Flues (18 by 5¼in)	281sq ft	Weight in working order	71 tons 1cwt
Total evaporative	1,157sq ft	Water capacity	2,000 gallons
Superheater (18 by 1.7/		Coal capacity	4 tons 10 cwt
32in)	197sq ft		
Total	1,354sq ft		

G Class 0-6-4T No.95 'Robert H. Selbie' at the coaling stage at Neasden, circa 1930. Named after the Met's energetic General Manager, this engine was built by the Yorkshire Engine Co at a cost of £3,621 and delivered on 30th December 1915. Like several other G Class locomotives, No.95 sustained cracked frames and was out of service from August 1927 until July 1928, when the frames were renewed and a new boiler was fitted. Sold to the LNER, where it became Class 'M2' No.6155, in November 1937, it was renumbered 9076 under the 1946 scheme and withdrawn from service in October 1948, before carrying the British Railways number, 69076. Lens of Sutton

G Class 0-6-4T No.97 'Brill', photographed at Aylesbury on May 1st 1937, six months before its sale to the LNER, and lettered 'London Transport'. Built by the Yorkshire Engine Co. in 1916 at a cost of £3,956, No.97 and its three sisters were chiefly used on freight trains. No.97 received a new boiler during an overhaul by Kerr Stuart at Stoke-on-Trent in 1929, having acquired the boiler from *H Class* 4-4-4T No.106 six years earlier. The 'London Transport' lettering was probably applied in 1934, when it received the boiler from No.96. Renumbered 6157 by the LNER, it was withdrawn in 1943. J.M. Jarvis

They had Robinson superheaters and Wakefield mechanical lubricators, the first Metropolitan locomotives to carry these refinements. Boilers were very similar to those used later in the 'H' Class 4-4-4 tanks of 1920, but had a slightly smaller heating surface. The superheaters originally had draught retarders, but these were later replaced by a pair of Maunsell snifting valves; safety valves were of the Ramsbottom type. The coal rails on the bunkers sloped inwards to allow for circular windows in the rear of the cabs, which had sliding plates over the lookouts at the cab sides, though these plates were apparently not fitted until after delivery, as a photograph of No.94 in June 1916 shows the engine without this feature. All four engines received names, the first named Metropolitan steam locomotives since Beyer Peacock 'A' Class 4-4-0 tanks Nos.1 to 18 briefly bore names from Greek mythology in the 1860s. These were 94 'Lord Aberconway' (Chairman of the Metropolitan), 95 'Robert H. Selbie' (the General Manager), 96 'Charles Jones' (Chief Mechanical Engineer, who nominally designed the locomotives), and 97 'Brill', presumably chosen because it was the most far-flung outpost served by the railway. Nameplates were of cast brass, curved to the contour of the front coupled-wheel splashers.

On 15th June 1928 Selbie wrote to George Hally, who had succeeded Charles Jones as Chief Mechanical Engineer five years earlier, expressing concern at the fact that No.95 had been in the workshops at Neasden awaiting repair since August 1927, and No.94 since January 1928; this was causing a heavy loss to the company. Hally replied that both engines had frames cracked right through; these had been replaced; No.95 had been fitted with a new boiler also, and would be back in service in about a week's time. No.94, however, needed a new boiler, superheater tubes, piston heads, piston valves, bogie castings and axleboxes, plus several small items, and he estimated the total cost as not far short of £5,000. It was hoped to have it back in service by about the end of October. He stated that Nos.96 and 97 also had cracked frames, and boilers which were reaching the end of their useful lives.

Selbie replied that if repairs to Nos.96 and 97 were going to be as expensive as in the case of No.94, it might be better to obtain tenders from outside. Hally revised his estimate for repairs to No.94 to the figure of £3,336, but in October 1928 he wrote to Beyer Peacock, Kerr Stuart, Hudswell Clarke and the Yorkshire Engine Co to ask if they could repair No.96, and if so, at what cost.

Beyer Peacock were too busy, and Hudswell Clarke said that as the full nature of the repairs necessary would not be known until the engine was stripped down, they would like to discuss the matter with Hally. The Yorkshire Engine Co, however, did put in an offer, quoting a price not exceeding £1,230, plus £130 for new cylinders and £300 if repairs were needed to tanks, bunker and cab. Completion of the work would be in 12 to 16 weeks. Kerr Stuart offer was £2,101, with some material to be supplied by the Metropolitan. Hally favoured Kerr Stuart as he said they had much better plant and equipment than the Yorkshire Engine Co, and so their offer was accepted on 15th November 1928, completion to be in about 12 weeks, and No.96 and the material supplied by Neasden were sent to Kerr Stuart on 24th November. When the engine was stripped down Kerr Stuart asked for an additional £81-4-7d for extra work, but they settled for half of this amount.

On 15th February 1929 Hally wrote to W. Holt, the Metropolitan's Traffic Manager, summarising the position regarding the four 'G' Class locomotives. No.94 had broken cylinders and would be out of service until the end of April; No.95 was back in service; No.96 should return from Kerr Stuart in about a fortnight, and No.97 had a flawed crank axle. No.96 arrived back from Kerr Stuart on 1st March 1929; the final bill was for £1,239-4-4d, considerably less than the figure of £2,101 which they had quoted, but this latter amount probably included new cylinders and other material which, in the event, the Metropolitan supplied themselves.

On several occasions 'G' Class boilers were exchanged between different engines; No.94 received the boiler from No.95 in 1921; No.96 received the boiler from No.95 in December 1933, and No.97 received the boiler from No.96 in December 1934, having previously received the boiler from 'H' Class 4-4-4 tank No.106 in September 1923. No.95 received the boiler from No.106 in August 1932. A new boiler made by Kerr Stuart was fitted to No.96 in 1920; this engine was weighed on the LNER weighbridge at Neasden ex-GCR shed in 1935 after trouble with a hot axlebox.

In 1937 London Transport, who had absorbed the Metropolitan on 1st July 1933, wished to rebuild Neasden Works and use the space occupied by the engine sheds for new car sheds, so they agreed with the LNER that the latter should take over responsibility for working Metropolitan Line goods services and the passenger services north of Rickmansworth from 1st November 1937. On that date the three classes of larger Metropolitan locomotives ('G' Class 0-6-4T, 'H' Class 4-4-4T and 'K' Class 2-6-4T) were sold to the LNER and transferred to Neasden ex-Great Central shed. Their crews went with them into LNER service and even kept in their own links, wearing their own distinctive uniforms. The Metropolitan was a company with great esprit de corps, and they still referred to themselves as 'Met men'. A small engine shed was built by London Transport at Neasden to house the smaller Metropolitan engines which they retained for working permanent way trains and certain goods duties.

The four 'G' Class engines were overhauled at Stratford, emerging in unlined black livery. Various minor modifications were carried out while in LNER ownership; during World War II they were altered to conform to the LNER loading gauge and Great Central pattern chimneys were fitted, though these did not greatly alter their appearance. At the same time, the dome and cab were reduced in height. Those locomotives which had not already received Ross pop safety valves in place of the original Ramsbottom pattern while in Metropolitan ownership had this modification made by the LNER. Nos.94, 95 and 97 had Maunsell pattern smokebox doors fastened with six circumferential clips when taken over, and No.94 retained this for a while under LNER ownership as No.6154. The 'G' Class engines, which became LNER Class 'M2', also retained, at least for some years, the trip cock gear which was fitted to all locomotives which worked over London Transport lines. These tripcocks automatically applied the brakes if a train passed a signal at danger, by engaging with a train-stop at track level.

In 1937 the 'G' Class locomotives became LNER Nos. 6154-6157; under the 1946 scheme they were renumbered as shown below. No.97 was withdrawn in 1943 and so was never allocated a 1946 number, and No.94, though allocated No.9075, never carried it. The two engines which survived to be taken over by British Railways never carried the BR numbers allotted to them.

Although mixed traffic engines, the 'G' Class were rarely used on passenger train duties in Metropolitan and LPTB days. Early in 1938, while the 'H' Class 4-4-4 tanks were being overhauled at Stratford, their employment on passenger work became more frequent, and this also obtained after World War II when arrears of maintenance created shortages of motive power on the LNER.

They were withdrawn as follows:–

Met & LPTB No.	1937 LNER No.	1946 LNER No.	BR No.	Withdrawn
94	6154	(9075)	-	May 1946
95	6155	9076	(69076)	Oct 1948
96	6156	9077	(69077)	Oct 1948
97	6157	-	-	Jan 1943

They remained at Neasden LNER shed throughout their time in LNER and British Railways ownership, and continued to be employed on the Metropolitan line duties for which they were originally built.

In an article in the March 1976 'SLS Journal' Mr C.B. Harley, who worked for the Yorkshire Engine Co, stated that six 'G' Class engines were ordered by the Metropolitan. This conflicts with the entries in the Board minutes, which clearly state that two engines were ordered in September 1914, and two more in January 1915. But the running numbers 98 and 99 were left vacant, which does suggest that six engines in all were contemplated. Any information as to why the last two engines were never built would be very welcome.

Early in 1929 'G' Class No.94 was fitted with Trofinoff By-Passing Piston Valves, the first British locomotive to be so equipped. These valves were manufactured at Neasden Works to drawings supplied by Messrs C. Frenkel (the patents were later taken over by the TAB Engineering Co). The object of this type of piston valve was to provide a by-pass of generous cross-section to connect the opposite ends of the cylinder when the engine was coasting. This was achieved by the heads not being fixed on the valve spindle, but having freedom to slide between two collars on the spindle. When the regulator was opened the pressure of the steam thus admitted held the valve heads as far apart as the collars permitted, and the valve thus worked in the ordinary way as it would if it were solid. But when steam was shut off the motion of the valve spindles pushed the valve heads towards the middle of the steam chest, where they remained until steam was readmitted. This meant that when the engine was coasting, air could pass freely from either end of the cylinder to the other, and so there was little resistance to drifting.

'The Locomotive Magazine' for 15th December 1930 reported that No.94 had been working continuously on passenger and goods train services for seventeen months, and showed a distinct improvement in its ability to run more freely and ride more steadily; considerable economies in coal and oil consumption were recorded, the saving in coal being about 9%. The article in the 'Locomotive Magazine' states that six further Metropolitan locomotives were being equipped with these TAB piston valves; it does not say which these were, but they must have been of the 'G', 'H' or 'K' classes, as earlier types would have had flat valves, and so it would not have been possible to convert them.

The LNER later equipped some ex-Great Central 'Director' Class 4-4-0 engines with TAB valves.

H Class 4-4-4T No.103, the first of a class of eight engines built by Kerr Stuart & Co, and delivered on 7th October 1920 at a cost of £11,575. Curved handrails from the front buffer-beam to the footplate above the cylinders have not yet been fitted, nor have the sliding shutters to the cabside openings. The lettering is in the original style, and No.103 carries the original large brass maker's plates on the smokebox saddle, which read, rather curiously, 'Kerr Stuarts, London', although the works was at Stoke-on-Trent. Note footsteps on front and rear buffer-beams. Boilers of *G* and *H Class* engines were interchangeable, and No.103 received the boiler from *G Class* No.94 in 1923, from *H Class* No.105 in 1931, and from *G Class* No.97 in 1935. It became LNER *Class H2* No.6415 in November 1937, was transferred to Colwick Shed, Nottingham in December 1941, and was withdrawn in March 1946 before carrying the 1946 scheme number, 7510, allocated to it.
London Transport Museum

10 **H Class 4-4-4 Tanks**

In 1915 the Metropolitan Railway began forward planning to promote greater passenger traffic in the undeveloped rural areas of Middlesex, Hertfordshire and Buckinghamshire through which the Aylesbury line passed, and the name 'Metro-Land' was coined as a means of publicising this aim. It is characteristic of Robert H. Selbie, their energetic and enterprising General Manager, that he should be planning expanding services even during the Great War. These improved services and accelerated timings would need new locomotives to work them; apart from the four 'G' Class 0-6-4 tanks, which by 1917 were causing problems with cracked main frames and a proneness to derailing in sidings, the company's most modern passenger engines were the 'E' Class 0-4-4Ts, built at the turn of the century and rather underpowered for hauling six-coach trains to faster timings over the undulating Aylesbury line.

In December 1917 Neasden drawing office produced a design for a proposed outside cylinder 4-4-4 tank engine with the drive onto the rear coupled wheels and long side tanks. This was not proceeded with, but in January 1919 a specification was drawn up for eight 4-4-4 tank locomotives. These were to

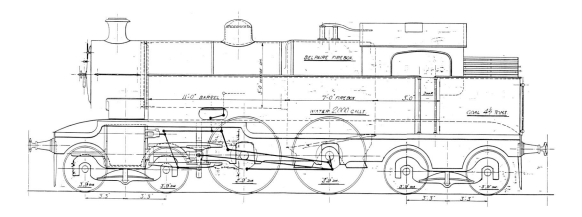

A Neasden drawing of 1917 for a 4-4-4 tank engine with drive onto rear coupled wheels and long side tanks. Courtesy National Railway Museum

General Arrangement of 'H' Class 4-4-4T, built by Kerr, Stuart & Co., 1920.
Courtesy National Railway Museum

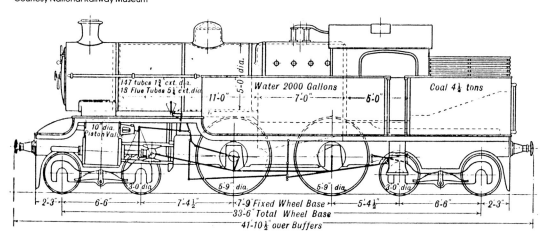

employ the same boiler and bogie as the 'G' Class 0-6-4T, and should be capable of hauling 250-ton trains at an average speed of 35mph between Wembley Park and Verney Junction. Bearing in mind the tendency of the 'G' Class engines to derail in sidings, it was stipulated that the new engines should be capable of safely negotiating yard curves of 4½ chains radius.

The Metropolitan invited tenders from the North British Locomotive Co, Hawthorn Leslie, the Yorkshire Engine Co and Kerr Stuart & Co for these engines, which were to the broad design of Charles Jones, the Metropolitan's Chief Mechanical Engineer. The North British Locomotive Co could not tender for this design, but said they could do so for engines of the Caledonian Railway Pickersgill 4-6-2T type or the North British 4-4-2T design. They also said that if the North Eastern Railway would lend them drawings of their three-cylinder 4-4-4 tank engine, they could tender for this type for the Metropolitan. Hawthorn Leslie's price was lower than that of Kerr Stuart, but they could not promise a delivery date or agree to a penalty clause for late delivery.

Kerr Stuarts' price was £11,800 per engine, and their tender for eight 4-4-4T engines was accepted and an order placed on 18th March 1919; they were to be delivered in 46 weeks from 1st May, with a penalty of £10 per engine per week for late delivery. The basis of the tender was later reduced to £9,800 per engine, plus an additional 1% for each shilling awarded as an increase in the weekly wage ratings during the currency of the contract. In May 1919 the price of steel was increased by £5 per ton,

An *H Class* 4-4-4 tank at Harrow-on-the-Hill on an Aylesbury train. It still has 'Metropolitan Railway' in curved lettering with the crest between; the date would be between 1920, when the *H Class* was delivered, and 1925, when electrification was extended to Rickmansworth, after which the change from electric to steam traction took place there. The second coach from the engine is 'Ashbury' low-roofed stock, while the other vehicles are of the later 'Dreadnought' type.

and Kerr Stuart asked for a corresponding increase in the contract price. Selbie, the Met General Manager, refused to agree to this, whereupon Kerr Stuart threatened to terminate the contract. After some lengthy and rather acrimonious correspondence, the Metropolitan finally agreed to bear this increased cost.

Kerr Stuart had submitted three alternative designs, all with the cylinders driving onto the *leading* coupled axle, with outside cylinders either 19in by 24in or 19in by 26in; the latter dimension was the one actually adopted. Some of the detailed design work seems to have been left to Kerr Stuart, as in June 1919 the Metropolitan requested a technical description of the new engines. Kerr Stuart were also asked to give the eight engines their final finish in Metropolitan livery.

The painting specification was as follows: Boiler, frames, tanks, bunkers, wheels and life guards – 2 coats lead colour, 5 coats of filling, well stopped and rubbed down, 2 coats lead colour, one coat 'Tuscan' red, one coat 'Midcared', one coat of glaze, picked out, written and lined, and 3 coats best English copal varnish.

On 22nd September 1919 Kerr Stuart wrote to say that their moulders had gone on strike, which might delay delivery. There was also delay in their receiving Yorkshire iron plates for the eight boilers and one spare boiler, and these plates did not arrive at Kerr Stuart's works until February 1920. The completed locomotives were delivered as follows:

	Works No.	*Delivered*
No.103	4088	7/10/20
104	4089	22/10/20
105	4090	3/11/20
106	4091	24/11/20
107	4092	10/3/21
108	4093	14/4/21
109	4094	11/6/21
110	4095	23/6/21

H Class 4-4-4T No.105 taking water at Aylesbury on an 'up' train, about 1935. This engine was overhauled and repainted at Neasden in April 1934; at this time London Transport were undecided as to what fleet name they would adopt, so this engine and *F Class* No.91 were lettered 'MET.'

This view of *H Class* No.104 at Aylesbury on 2nd May 1936 shows very clearly the handsome lines of these engines; the tripcock gear between the leading bogie wheels can also be seen. H.C. Casserley

H Class 4-4-4T No.103 on a London train at Verney Junction in 1935. The line from Aylesbury to Verney Junction was opened in 1868 as the Aylesbury & Buckingham Railway, and absorbed by the Metropolitan on 1st July 1891. At Verney Junction it connected with the LNWR Oxford to Bletchley line. The Met operated through trains from this remote station (there was not even a village there) to Baker Street and the City, and even a Pullman service, but it was hardly surprising that London Transport withdrew the passenger services on 6th July 1936.
Photomatic

After deducting surcharges for increased steel and labour costs, the average cost worked out at £11,134 per locomotive, which did not allow for any profit by Kerr Stuart. On 28th July 1921 the Met board approved the payment of £11,134 per engine, plus 4% for profit, making a total of £11,575 per engine. The Metropolitan waived the interest on advance payments they had made to Kerr Stuart, and also the penalty for late delivery. Perhaps it was this generosity which prompted Kerr Stuart later to write to the Met saying what a pleasure it had been to do business with them – they must have forgotten their threat to cancel the contract earlier when the Met refused to pay the increased cost of steel. In 1922 the engines developed leaks in their side tanks, and the Metropolitan charged Kerr Stuart £10 per tank for rectifying this at Neasden.

Dimensions of the 'H' Class were:–

Cylinders (2 outside)	19in by 26in	Grate Area	21.4sq ft
Walschaerts valve gear		Weight in working order	78 tons 5cwt
with piston valves		Water Capacity	2,000 gallons
Coupled Wheels	5ft 9in diameter	Coal Capacity	4 tons 10cwt
Leading & trailing	3ft 0in diameter	Tractive Effort at 85%	18,500lbs
Wheels		pressure	
Boiler Pressure	160lbs		
Heating Surface:			
Firebox	132sq ft		
Tubes	744sq ft		
Flues	281sq ft		
Superheater	164sq ft		
Total	1,321sq ft		

H Class 4-4-4T No.106 on a six-coach train of 'Dreadnought' stock at Great Missenden, May 21st 1934, nearly a year after its acquisition by London Transport. It had received a new boiler supplied by Beyer Peacock four years earlier. In November 1937 it became LNER Class M2 No.6418; transferred to Colwick shed on December 4th 1941, it was withdrawn in May 1946, without carrying the 1946 number 7513 allotted to it. H.F. Wheeller

They were very handsome machines, the slightly-inclined cylinders driving the leading coupled wheels. The parallel boilers, of 5ft diameter with Belpaire fireboxes, had Ramsbottom safety valves, though these were later replaced by valves of the Ross pop type. The bunkers had coal rails which sloped inwards to accommodate circular look-outs in the backs of the cabs. When delivered, large oval Kerr Stuart works plates were fixed to the smokebox saddles but these were later removed, being replaced in some cases by smaller plates. Like the 'G' and 'K' classes, they had brackets for destination boards at front and rear, but, judging from photographic evidence, these boards were never carried. The 'H' class had footsteps on the front and rear buffer-beams. To assist enginemen in mounting the footplate, handrails were later fitted above the buffer-beams; these curved to join the footplating where it swept up over the cylinders. Sliding shutters were fitted to the cab side lookouts, but this appears to have been done later, as photographs of Nos.103, 104, 106 and 107 soon after delivery do not show this feature. Trip-cock apparatus was fitted some time after delivery, to the right-hand side of the leading bogie and to the left-hand side of the rear bogie.

Little has been written about the performance of the 'H' Class, but their flexible wheelbase helped them to negotiate the curves on the Chesham branch, on which they worked the through trains from Baker Street. They had a good turn of speed, and had an opportunity to show this when working the 9.45am train from Aylesbury to Baker Street. Before 1925, when electrification was extended to Rickmansworth, this train ran non-stop over the 19.6 miles between Great Missenden and Harrow, and 'Locomotives of the LNER', Part 7 (RCTS) says they sometimes attained 75mph down Chorley

Wood bank. They practically monopolised the Metropolitan passenger trains north of Harrow, and, after electrification was extended in 1925, north of Rickmansworth. Before the arrival of the 'K' Class 2-6-4 tanks, 'H' Class engines were sometimes used on goods trains, when the load was limited to 285 tons, but this caused overheating of tyres owing to braking stresses. This was another factor which led to the ordering of the 'K' Class 2-6-4 tanks.

In 1920 there was a coal strike, and No.108 was experimentally fitted with the Scarab oil-burning apparatus. A report by Charles Jones early in 1921 had stated that the cost of coal firing of locomotives (presumably on an annual basis) was £48,060, whereas oil firing, including conversion of locomotives and provision of an oil storage tank, would be £84,713. However, the price of oil was reduced in April 1921 and Selbie evidently felt that the conversion of one engine, No.108, would be worth a trial. So the Scarab Oil Burning Co supplied an oil tank, burner etc for £145-0-0. Some other parts for the conversion were supplied by the Metropolitan, at a cost of about £60-0-0. The tank was rectangular, 4ft by 4ft by 4ft, holding 585 gallons, and fitted into the bunker. A photograph appeared in the 'Wonder Book of Railways' showing, erroneously, No.106 with the apparatus. This appears to be an official photograph, but the rectangular tank in the bunker has obviously been touched in; it is as tall as the cab roof eaves and has a circular filler at the top.

On 23rd August 1921 Jones wrote to the Scarab company to say that No.108 was again out of service with a defective brick arch. Its running had been anything but satisfactory. And on 12th December he asked Scarab to make an offer to buy back the apparatus, which had been removed from the locomotive. Two boilers at Neasden Power Station had also been equipped on the Scarab system, but its use had been discontinued, for economic reasons. The Scarab company were not interested in buying back the equipment, and so Selbie instructed the Met Stores Superintendent to dispose of it when possible.

An interesting view of *H Class* 4-4-4 tank No.107 at Aylesbury on July 5th 1934, either shunting or at the head of a goods train, both unusual duties for this class at this period, although before the arrival of the *K Class* 2-6-4Ts, *H Class* engines were sometimes employed on freight duties. N. Shepherd

A spate of hot axleboxes occurred in 1924, mainly to 'H' Class engines; Hally, who had taken over as Chief Mechanical Engineer the previous year, thought this was due to overloading, and suggested to Selbie that a locomotive weighbridge be provided at Neasden so that loading on individual axles could be measured. Selbie replied that this would be very expensive and asked what the practice was on other railways. Hally ascertained that a weighbridge would cost about £6,000, and he did not think that so large a sum would be saved by the elimination of hot axleboxes. He therefore inspected the weighbridge at Neasden LNER shed, and he was able to arrange for Metropolitan locomotives to have their axle weights checked there.

Detailed alterations to the 'H' Class included the substitution, from 1933 onwards, of Ross Pop safety-valves for the original Ramsbottom pattern, and smoke-box doors secured by circumferential dog clips instead of a central dart and handle.

In common with the 'G' and 'K' Classes, the 'H' Class engines were sold to the LNER in November 1937, when the latter company took over the responsibility for Metropolitan Line steam-hauled services. They were classified 'H2' by the LNER, where they became Nos.6415 to 6422. In the spring of 1938 they were sent to Stratford Works for overhaul, emerging in unlined black livery. On return to Neasden GCR shed they continued to be employed on Metropolitan Line passenger trains north of Rickmansworth.

The last locomotive to be overhauled at the Neasden locomotive works before they were closed and the larger engines sold to the LNER was 'H' Class No.103, which had a general repair and repaint on 24th August 1937.

Working pressure was increased to 170lb per sq inch in 1941, which boosted the tractive effort at 85% boiler pressure to 19,656lb. Starting in the same year, the class were fitted with shorter chimneys and lower domes, while the cab roofs were lowered. The new chimneys, of Great Central pattern, did not greatly alter the appearance of the engines, however.

In December 1941 all eight engines were transferred to the Nottingham area. They were allocated to Colwick shed, though 6420/1/2 were at Langwith for a while and were used on the LD&EC line Lincoln to Chesterfield services. At Colwick they worked the Nottingham suburban trains; the Colwick crews did not like them very much, though this may have simply been due to the conservatism of enginemen when faced with an unfamiliar type of locomotive.

Under the 1946 renumbering scheme they became Nos.7510 to 7516, 6421 having been withdrawn from Langwith in 1942 and thus not being allocated a 1946 number. In fact, only 6416 and 6417 actually carried their new numbers. Their allocations on transfer, and withdrawal dates were as shown in the table below.

Met. Rly. & LPTB No.	1937 LNER No.	1946 No.	Allocation on Transfer	Withdrawn
103	6415	(7510)	Colwick 6/12/41	Mar 1946
104	6416	7511	Colwick 5/12/41	Nov 1947
105	6417	7512	Colwick 7/12/41	Oct 1947
106	6418	(7513)	Colwick 4/12/41	May 1946
107	6419	(7514)	Colwick 5/12/41	Sep 1943
108	6420	(7515)	Langwith 12/12/41	
			Colwick 14/8/42	May 1946
109	6421	–	Colwick 6/12/41	
			Langwith 12/12/41	Apr 1942
110	6422	(7516)	Colwick 4/12/41	
			Langwith 12/12/41	
			Colwick 18/7/42	May 1946

The withdrawal of No.104 as LNER 7511 in November 1947 saw the end of what I always felt to be the most handsome and characteristic of the modern Metropolitan locomotives; they ended their days in dirty black, but in their heyday, like all Metropolitan engines, they were kept spotlessly clean, and their dark red livery contrasted well with the varnished teak of the 'Dreadnought' stock.

Nos.104 and 107 received new boilers supplied by the Avonside Engine Co in 1933; in 1931 a new Beyer Peacock boiler was fitted to No.106, and No.110 had a new boiler made by Kerr Stuart in 1923. Boilers were also exchanged between different members of the 'H' Class from time to time.

K Class 2-6-4T No.113 on an 'up' freight train at Aylesbury, circa 1930. Next to the locomotive are two private owners' wagons, of a type which made goods trains full of colour and variety in the years before World War II.

11 K Class 2-6-4 Tanks

In a report to the Board in 1924 Selbie stated the necessity of obtaining goods engines of greater power, so that fewer, longer freight trains could be worked than could be handled by existing locomotives. At that time the only true goods engines the company owned were the four small 'F' Class 0-6-2 tanks; the 'G' Class 0-6-4Ts were mixed traffic engines, but there were only four of them. What Selbie had in mind was probably decreasing line occupancy by goods trains so that when electric traction was extended to Rickmansworth, which was then in hand, a faster and more frequent passenger service could be operated. The specification for the new locomotives called for them to be capable of hauling 600 tons at 35mph on the level and at 25mph up a gradient of 1 in 94.

After the end of the First World War a number of 2-6-0 locomotives, generally similar to Maunsell's 'N' Class design for the South Eastern & Chatham Railway, had been manufactured at Woolwich Arsenal, to provide employment there as the demand for munitions decreased. These engines were offered for sale by the George Cohen & Armstrong Disposals Corporation, and on 23rd July 1924 the Metropolitan signed a contract with the Corporation for the supply of parts for six locomotives, to have frames lengthened at the rear to take a trailing bogie and to have side tanks and a bunker fitted. The conversion work, to the design of George Hally, who had succeeded Charles Jones as Met Chief Mechanical Engineer in 1923, was to be carried out by Sir W.G. Armstrong Whitworth & Co at their

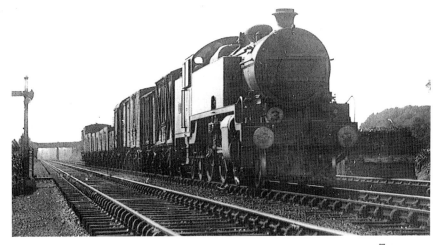

K Class 2-6-4T No.116 on a Verney Junction to Harrow goods train near Chalfont, 18th June 1933, twelve days before the Met was absorbed by London Transport. This is the No.3 Goods train; it has left Verney Junction at 8.10am and after shunting and clearing sidings at all stations to Rickmansworth and Watford will finally reach Harrow at 9.40pm.
LCGB Ken Nunn Collection

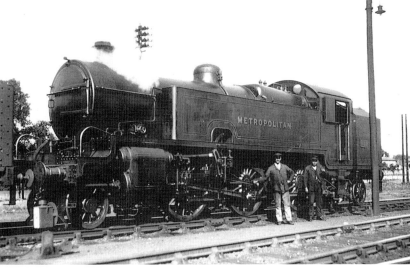

The crew of K Class 2-6-4 tank No.111 stand proudly in front of their engine. The background suggests that the location is Aylesbury.

Scotswood Works, Newcastle, and the completed locomotives would cost £5,000 each. This was remarkably cheap, as Kerr Stuart's tender for the 'H' Class 4-4-4 tanks four years previously was £11,800 each, but the Disposals Corporation was probably anxious to obtain a sale. In the event their actual cost was even less, at £4,729-3-9 each.

The contract called for delivery of the locomotives by 19th September but, in fact, they were not completed until early in 1925, as follows:

Met. No.	Armstrong Whitworth Works No.	Delivery date	Into Traffic
111	702	19/1/25	21/3/25
112	703	19/1/25	21/3/25
113	704	28/1/25	23/3/25
114	705	28/1/25	23/3/25
115	706	11/2/25	28/3/25
116	707	11/2/25	28/3/25

The Metropolitan decided not to press for a penalty for the delay in delivery; their solicitor advised them that this could only have been for a nominal amount, as they were unable to prove that serious inconvenience had been caused.

The taper boilers, built by George Stephenson & Co at Darlington had top feed on the domes, Ross pop safety valves and chimneys with capuchons, a feature not found on other Metropolitan locomotives. The leading pony trucks were of the Cartazzi sliding type, with spherical centres, and the trailing bogies were standard with those on the 'G' Class 0-6-4 Tanks and 'H' Class 4-4-4Ts. Length over buffers was 44ft 10¾in, and they were designed to negotiate 4½ chain curves.

Another view of *K Class* 2-6-4 tank No.113 on a goods train at Aylesbury. The formation shown would have been well within its capabilities, as engines of the *G* and *K* classes were allowed in the working timetable to haul 600-ton trains between Verney Junction and Aylesbury. The wagons shown are a mixture of railway-owned and private-owner wagons. Passing to the LNER in 1937, No.113 became *Class L2* No.6160; renumbered 9071 in 1946, it survived until October 1948, the last of its class to be withdrawn. Dr Ian C. Allen

Other dimensions were as follows:–

Cylinders (2)	19in by 28in (Walschaerts valve gear; piston valves)	Grate Area	25sq ft
		Water Capacity	2,000 gallons
Coupled Wheels	5ft 6in diameter	Coal Capacity	4 tons
Bogie Wheels, front & rear	3ft 1in diameter	Weight in working order	87 tons 7 cwt
Boiler Pressure	200lb sq in	Tractive Effort (85%	
Heating Surface		pressure)	26,100lbs
Boiler	1,525.6sq ft		
Superheater	285sq ft		

Twin Maunsell-type snifting valves were fitted, one on each side of the smokebox. The smokebox doors were also of Maunsell pattern, secured by six dog clips round the edges. In common with the 'H' Class, the 'K' class had footsteps on the front and rear buffer beams, outside the buffers (there was no room for footsteps near the motion). To assist enginemen in mounting the footplate, handrails were fitted which curved from above the front buffer-beam to join the footplating where it was swept upwards over the cylinders. A feature which they shared with the 'G' and 'H' class engines was the provision of sliding shutters to the cab side openings. The coal bunkers sloped inwards at the top to allow for oval lookouts in the rear of the cab. They were fitted with trip cock apparatus for working over electrified lines; this was below the cylinders on the right-hand side, and under bunkers on the left-hand side.

In Metropolitan Railway days 'K' Class engines were usually confined to goods trains; in terms of hauling capacity they certainly met their specification, as the 1927 working timetable states that between Verney Junction and Aylesbury the No.3 Up Goods could be increased to 600 tons if worked by a 'G' or 'K' Class engine. This train left Verney Junction at 8.10am, calling and shunting at most stations as far as Rickmansworth and the Watford branch, and finally arrived at Harrow at 9.40pm.

Because of their dimensions, the 'K' Class were not allowed through the Finchley Road tunnels. There was some concern regarding their ability to clear station platform copings, and in February 1925 clearance tests were carried out. During these it was found that at Great Missenden, when passing over the crossover from the up to the down line at the London end, the cylinders only cleared the platform edge by ⅞in, and at Moor Park an engine grazed the platform coping. A note in the General Manager's papers however says, perhaps rather complacently, that where clearances were less than 3in this only occurred at places where the engine was moving slowly, so that no allowance need to be made for the rolling which applied at high speeds.

With their 5ft 6in coupled wheels, the 'K' Class would have been perfectly suitable for hauling passenger trains; that they seldom did so while in Metropolitan ownership was probably due to the fact that with eight 'H' Class 4-4-4 Tanks and four 'G' Class 0-6-4Ts, there was ample motive power already for these duties. The 'K' Class were the heaviest locomotives the Metropolitan possessed, and so they were used in October 1925 to test the deflection in the girders of the bridge over the River Gade on the Watford branch, during its Ministry of Transport inspection. Two engines were coupled together for this exercise, and seven years later a pair of 'K' Class engines were employed in consolidating the newly-laid track on the Stanmore branch.

As already mentioned, the London Passenger Transport Board, which had absorbed the Metropolitan on 1st July 1933, decided in 1937 to rebuild Neasden Works and car sheds, demolishing the old steam engine shed in the process. So on 1st November 1937 responsibility for working Metropolitan Line goods services and passenger trains beyond Rickmansworth was handed over to LNER, and at the same time the 'G', 'H' and 'K' class Metropolitan engines were sold to that company.

So the six 'K' Class engines moved to the former Great Central Railway shed at Neasden. In due course the 'H' Class 4-4-4 tanks were sent to Stratford Works for overhaul, and in 1938 this resulted in 'K' Class engines appearing on passenger trains. In April that year I saw several instances of this, and also of LNER 'A5' 4-6-2 tank engines on purely London Transport passenger trains. In 1942 the transfer of the 'H' Class (now LNER 'H2') locomotives to the Nottingham area brought another shortage of motive power, and once again 'K' Class engines filled the breach on Metropolitan Line passenger duties. This continued in the post-war period.

After their acquisition by the LNER the 'K' Class were overhauled at Stratford Works, and emerged in unlined black livery. They became LNER Class 'L2'. While in LNER ownership there were certain detail alterations, such as the substitution of LNER pattern lamp irons for the original Metropolitan pattern, but they were not fundamentally altered. They were renumbered 6158 to 6163, Nos.6161 and 6163 not receiving their new numbers until November 1938. When the 1946 renumbering scheme was introduced, only four engines still existed, and only two of these actually bore their new numbers, as follows:–

Met. & LPTB No.	1937 No.	1946 No.	Withdrawn
111	6158	9070	Oct 1948
112	6159	-	Jan 1943
113	6160	9071	Oct 1948
114	6161	-	May 1943
115	6162	(9072)	Jan 1946
116	6163	(9073)	May 1945

Loco's 9072 and 9073 never bore their new numbers; 9070 and 9071 were allocated the addition of 60,000 to their numbers by British Railways, but were withdrawn before this could be applied. The 'K' Class remained at Neasden LNER shed until withdrawn.

Manning Wardle 0-6-0ST at Quainton Road circa 1900. Originally named 'Earl Temple', it was acquired new by the Oxford & Aylesbury Tramroad in 1894. It subsequently became 'Brill No.2', but was later renamed 'Brill No.1'. It was taken over by the Metropolitan in 1899 when they assumed responsibility for working the Brill branch, and was sold to T.W. Ward of Sheffield in 1915; they resold it to Frank Hayes, a contractor, who used it on constructing the Great West Road. Later it passed to Kirk & Randall, of Bromborough, Cheshire. A typical Manning Wardle product of their K Class, it appears to be in Met dark red livery though not bearing the company's name; there was probably no space to put it in! LCGB Ken Nunn Collection

12 Miscellaneous Locomotives

In March 1883 the Metropolitan purchased from B.N. Smith & Son, the contractor building part of Neasden Works, an 0-4-0 tank engine, for shunting within the works. Little is known about this locomotive, but the Met paid £200 for it. In 1886 they sold it to W. Maxwell, the contractor for the Pinner to Rickmansworth extension, for £500, plus £107-11-1 for repairs that were necessary, so they made a handsome profit on this transaction. It was Metropolitan No.75, and to replace it the Met purchased a new 0-4-0 saddle tank (No.100) from Hudswell, Clarke (Works No.253 of 1886). Outside cylinders were 13in by 20in and coupled wheels 3ft 3in diameter; weight in working order was only 22 tons. It had a stovepipe chimney and, when delivered, a graceful curved safety-valve column over the firebox. This was later replaced by a brass dome with spring-balance safety valves, and the weatherboard, which had been bent backwards at the top, was extended to form a rudimentary cab. It was withdrawn in 1907, and sold four years later to Robert Fraser & Sons of Newcastle for £75.

In 1905 the Metropolitan acquired a Manning Wardle 0-6-0 saddle tank, 'Nellie', built in 1867 (Works No.23). This had been used by Bott & Stennet, the contractors for the Uxbridge branch, who had acquired it after it had passed through the hands of five other owners. It appears to have been hired by the Met, as no reference has been found to its purchase in the Met Minutes, and the fact that it was never given a Metropolitan running number seems to bear this out. It was a typical Manning Wardle product, with square riveted saddle tank, a fluted safety valve column and a weather board bent backwards at the top to give a little protection to the enginemen. Inside cylinders were 12in by 17in and coupled wheels were 3ft diameter, with weight in working order 16¾ tons. It was rebuilt in 1891 with a new boiler, firebox and chimney. It was used for shunting at Neasden and Wembley Park, and by using a match truck with suitable couplings at either end it could be used for marshalling trains of electric stock. It was the only engine light enough to work over a bridge within Neasden Works which crossed over the River Brent, but this bridge was rebuilt in 1908, and the installation of overhead conductors within the Electric Car Shed in 1916 made its use for making up electric trains no longer necessary. It was withdrawn in 1915.

Three very similar 0-6-0 saddle tanks were acquired by the Metropolitan when it took over the working of the Brill branch in 1899. 'Huddersfield No.1', built in 1876, was a Manning Wardle 'K' Class engine, Works No.616, and was purchased by the Oxford & Aylesbury tramroad, owners of the Brill branch, in 1894. It was later renamed 'Wotton No.1'. Another 'K' Class engine, 'Earl Temple', Manning Wardle No.1249, was bought new in 1894; it was subsequently renamed 'Brill No.2', but later renumbered 'Brill No.1'. A third 0-6-0ST, 'Wotton No.2', Manning Wardle No.1415, was purchased, probably new, in February 1899, just before the Metropolitan took over.

'Wotton No.1' was sold to Phillips, Emlyn Works, Newport, Mon, in 1901, but the other two engines continued to work on the Brill branch for a few years, until replaced by Metropolitan 'D' Class 2-4-0 tanks Nos.71 and 72. They were both sold to T.W. Ward Ltd of Sheffield in 1915 for £300. 'Brill No.1' was resold to Frank Hayes, a London-based contractor, who used it on construction of the Great West Road. Later it passed to Kirk & Randall, of Bromborough. 'Wotton No.2' went to Holland, Hannen & Cubitts, who resold it later to C.J. Wills & Co of Chadwell Heath, Essex.

Dimensions of all three engines were:–

Cylinders (inside)	12in by 17in	Weight in working order	16¾ tons
Total Heating Surface	370sq ft	Coupled Wheels:	
Wheelbase	10ft 9in	'Wotton No.1'	3ft 1⅜in diameter
Grate Area	7sq ft	'Brill No.1 and	
Capacity of Water Tank	450 gallons	'Wotton No.2'	3ft diameter

Details of all three locomotives were broadly similar, but 'Wotton No.1' had only a weatherboard bent backwards at the top to give the enginemen a little protection and its smokebox door was horizontally hinged, whereas the other two engines had canopies over their footplates and circular smokebox doors hinged at the side. 'Brill No.1' and 'Wotton No.2' had spark arresters and were fitted with governors to regulate speed; they also had straight combined name and number plates, fixed to the saddle tanks.

Manning Wardle 0-6-0ST 'Nellie', built 1867. After passing through several other owners, it was acquired by Bott & Stennett, contractors who built the Metropolitan's Uxbridge branch. After this was opened in July 1904, Bott & Stennett hired 'Nellie' to the Met, who used it for shunting at Neasden and Wembley Park and, in conjunction with a match truck with suitable couplings at each end, for marshalling electric stock. It was the only engine light enough to pass over a bridge over the River Brent within Neasden Works. This bridge was strengthened in 1908, and later, overhead conductors were installed in the Electric Car Shed to facilitate the making up of trains. This rendered 'Nellie' redundant, and it was withdrawn from service in 1915. The fluted safety valve column betrays its early origin; it retained this when given a new boiler in 1891. LCGB Ken Nunn Collection

Manning Wardle 0-6-0ST 'Wotton No.2' at Brill, 2nd August 1909. This was purchased by the Oxford & Aylesbury Tramroad in February 1899, just before the Metropolitan took over the working of the Brill Branch. Fitted with a new boiler in 1914, it was sold a year later to T.W. Ward of Sheffield. They disposed of it to Holland, Hannen & Cubitts, and it later passed to C.J. Wills & Co of Chadwell Heath, Essex. LCGB Ken Nunn

0-4-0ST No.100, built by Hudswell Clarke in 1886, and purchased new by the Metropolitan in that year. This engine, which only weighed 22 tons in working order, was used for shunting and marshalling coaching stock at Neasden. When delivered it had a curved safety valve column over the firebox instead of the dome shown here, and only a weather board, bent back at the top, as protection for the enginemen. It was withdrawn in 1907, and sold to Robert Fraser & Sons of Newcastle four years later. L&GRP

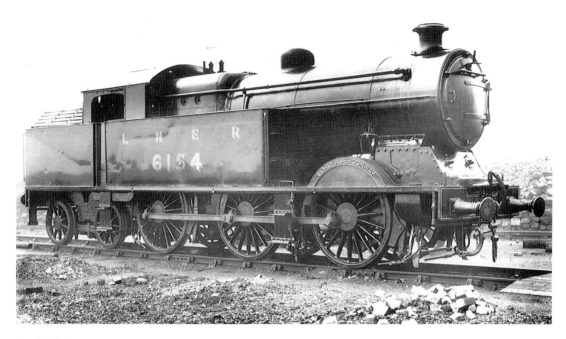

An official photograph taken at Stratford on a rather dull day in October 1941 of LNER *M2 Class* 0-6-4T No.6154. Formerly Met No.94 of *Class G*, it retains its name, 'Lord Aberconway', but a Great Central chimney and a lower dome have been fitted. This was presumably done so that these engines could work over other sections of the LNER, but as far as is known, they remained at Neasden ex-GCR engine shed until withdrawn. A smokebox door fastened with clips round its circumference has been substituted for the original pattern, which had a central locking handle. No.6154 had probably just been overhauled.

13 **The LNER Locomotives**

The New Works Programme, 1935-1940, for the railways of London included the projection of Bakerloo Line trains over the Metropolitan Stanmore branch, via a new tube link from Finchley Road to Baker Street. When completed, this would involve the stabling of Bakerloo Line rolling stock at Neasden Depot, necessitating additional car sheds. In order to make space for these, London Transport wanted to demolish the old Met steam locomotive shed. In its turn, this would mean disposing of the larger ex-Metropolitan steam locomotives, and making some new arrangements for the working of LPTB steam trains north of Rickmansworth, together with freight trains on the Metropolitan & Great Central Joint line and the Watford and Uxbridge branches.

It was decided to approach the London & North Eastern Railway, who since 1923 had been partners in the Met & GC Joint Committee and who had a steam locomotive depot at Neasden, to ask if they were prepared to take over these workings. A meeting was held at Liverpool Street LNER station on 28th May 1937 between an LNER party led by V.M. Barrington-Ward (Superintendent, Western Section) and an LPTB team headed by George Hally (Operating Manager, Railways, and formerly the Met's Chief Mechanical Engineer), and an agreement was drawn up on the following lines:

(1) The LNER was to work Goods and Coal trains serving the Met & GC Joint line and the Watford Joint Railway (this was Met & LNER Joint) on the same terms as the Transport Board were then receiving, i.e., 33⅓% of the Mileage Receipts, plus 15s 10d per engine hour and 2s per guard hour for shunting, both subject to a coal and water clause. It was stipulated that if the working of freight trains was retarded by the extension of electrification to Amersham and increased electric services north of Harrow, the figure of 33⅓% of the mileage receipts was to be reviewed.

(2) The LNER to provide locomotive power for LPTB passenger trains north of Rickmansworth, for which they would receive 25s 0.93d per engine hour, subject to a coal and water clause.

(3) The LNER was to take over the working of freight traffic to and from LPTB stations between Baker Street, Harrow and Uxbridge, at a rate of 19s 11.76d per engine hour subject to a coal and water clause, and 2s per hour for guards.

(4) The LNER to take over certain rolling stock belonging to the LPTB.

(5) Certain of the Transport Board staff were to be transferred on loan to the LNER.

(6) An additional shed road, engine pits, water and other facilities would be constructed at Neasden LNER Depot to accommodate the transferred locomotives, at an estimated cost of £2,330. The interest on the capital for these works had been included in calculating the rate to be paid to the LNER for working LPTB freight trains.

The agreement in Paragraph 1 regarding shunting stated that the LNER would take over the shunting duties at Harrow on a permanent basis; hitherto these had been undertaken by the Metropolitan and the Great Central (LNER after 1923) in alternate five-year periods. It is interesting that among the smaller engines retained by the LPTB however were the two Peckett 0-6-0 saddle tanks, one of which had usually been employed on this duty.

LPTB steam working staff loaned to the LNER would have the option of re-transfer to the Board's electric train staff as vacancies occurred or as electrification of further steam lines proceeded. They would be supplied with uniforms by the Transport Board and cap badges would read 'MET & LNER'. They would continue to serve under LPTB conditions of service and rates of pay. Positions available would be advertised to Met steam staff of all grades, and the senior applicants would be transferred.

Staff transferred would be confined to the particular work transferred, and would work only on Met, Met & GC and Watford Joint lines, and the LNER lines between Harrow and Neasden. (It is not known whether this still applied when the 'H' Class 4-4-4 tanks were transferred to the Nottingham area in 1941, but wartime requirements would probably have applied and the footplate staff would have been transferred along with their engines.)

As part of the agreement the LNER undertook to fit tripcocks to any of their engines which were required to work over the Metropolitan Line proper. They also agreed to hire locomotives to the LPTB for hauling ballast trains, but it is doubtful if this was ever necessary, as the Board had retained eleven of the smaller Met engines for these duties.

The agreement was duly authorised by the LPTB and the LNER directors, and embodied in a memorandum submitted to the Metropolitan & Great Central Joint Committee on 11th November 1937, signed by C.H. Newton, Divisional General Manager of the LNER, and J.P. Thomas, General Manager, Railways, of the LPTB. As the new arrangements had already been in operation since November 1st, the Joint Committee seems to have been presented with something of a fait accompli, but as it consisted of representatives of the LNER and London Transport, its approval was probably considered to be merely a formality.

The LPTB staff actually transferred to the LNER were 35 drivers, 36 firemen, 3 coalmen and 19 goods guards, making a total of 93.

LNER Class L2 2-6-4T No.6158, (formerly Met No.111) in dirty wartime condition at Neasden ex-Great Central shed in 1945. Apart from a few minor details these engines remained fundamentally unaltered while in LNER ownership. The first of the class, No.111 was delivered on 19th January 1925, became LNER 6158 in November 1937, and survived until October 1948, being renumbered 9070 under the 1946 LNER scheme. Photomatic Ltd

On the LNER the four 'G' Class 0-6-4Ts, Nos.94 to 97, became LNER Nos.6154 to 6157 of Class 'M2', the six 'K' Class 2-6-4Ts, Nos.111 to 116, became Class 'L2' Nos.6158 to 6163, and the eight 'H' Class 4-4-4Ts became Class 'H2' Nos.6415 to 6422. They were all duly overhauled at Stratford Works, and their subsequent history is told in Chapters 9, 10 and 11.

It is interesting to compare the prices paid for them by the LNER with those paid by the Metropolitan Railway when new. These are:–

	Delivered	Original Price (each)	Paid by LNER (each)
4 'G' Class 0-6-4T	1915 (2)	£3,621-0-0	£1,312-10-0 (36.25%)
	1916 (2)	£3,956-0-0	£1,312-10-0 (33.18%)
6 'K' Class 2-6-4T	1925	£4,729-3-9	£2,916-13-4 (61.67%)
8 'H' Class 4-4-4T	1920/21	£11,575-0-0	£1,625-0-0 (14.04%)

The high proportion of the original price which the LNER paid for the 'K' Class engines may be due to the fact that, being built from Government surplus parts, the original price was abnormally low. On the other hand, the 'H' Class locomotives, five years younger than the 'G' Class, realised only a small proportion of their original cost. The explanation, however, may be that the 4-4-4 tanks had been much more intensively used than the other two classes, as they worked practically all the Met steam-hauled passenger services. The 'G' Class were not often employed on passenger trains and the 'K' Class very rarely so; therefore with ten modern engines to handle freight trains, they had probably much less wear than the 4-4-4 tanks.

LNER Class M2 4-4-4T No.6416 (Met No.104) on a Mansfield train at Nottingham Victoria, June 18th 1946. It has a shorter chimney, and LNER group standard buffers and headlamp brackets have been substituted for the Metropolitan pattern. Transferred to Colwick shed on December 5th 1941, it survived long enough to carry its 1946 number, 7511, and was withdrawn in November 1947, the last survivor of its class. J.P. Wilson

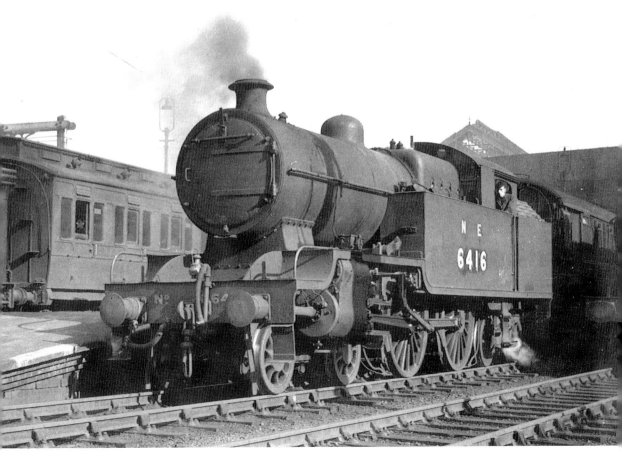

A view at Neasden engine shed on July 1st 1934, showing *F Class* 0-6-2T No.93, *A Class* 4-4-0T No.49 taking water, and *H Class* 4-4-4T No.104 at the coaling stage. Three men are giving some attention to the coupling rods of No.93. H.F. Wheeller

14 Neasden Works and Engine Shed

The Metropolitan's original locomotive works was at Chapel Street, Edgware Road, where there was also an engine shed. Some engines were rebuilt at this works, but the site was very cramped, and in 1880 some land was purchased on the up side of the line just north-west of what was then Kingsbury station (later renamed Neasden). Work on building a new works here began in February 1881; they included the Carriage Shop, Fitting and Turning Shop and other buildings. During 1882 Cowans Sheldon supplied a 50 ton traverser for use outside the Locomotive Shop, which was more spacious than the old premises at Edgware Road, and this permitted the rebuilding of many more engines than had previously been possible. Indeed, between 1894 and 1905 a total of 44 locomotives were rebuilt, all 'A' and 'B' Class 4-4-0 tanks. The new locomotive works was opened in 1883, and thirteen years later two 'E' Class 0-4-4T engines were built at Neasden, Nos.77 and 78, followed by 'E' Class No.1 two years later; these were the only locomotives actually built at Neasden.

The original engine sheds were at Edgware Road and Farringdon Street. When the line was extended to Harrow-on-the-Hill in 1880 a shed was opened there, but after the opening of the Neasden shed in 1883 this was closed and the shed building was moved to Neasden. There were also engine sheds at New Cross for the East London line traffic, at Chesham, Aylesbury, and a small timber shed at Brill.

The first engine shed at Neasden was a two-track building of wooden weatherboards with brick inspection pits and a water column; the shed building itself, as mentioned above, was transferred from Harrow; it accommodated 10 engines. In 1898 a new shed holding 20 engines was built; Joseph Firbank was the contractor for the foundations and locomotive pits. It was a roundhouse, the structure itself being built by Andrew Handyside & Co Ltd, over a 50ft turntable supplied by the Isca Foundry Co.

By 1908 this building was in a very poor state of repair, and shortly afterwards it was demolished by George Cohen, Sons & Co, who paid £185 for its scrap value.

After this the steam locomotives were housed in three roads of the Carriage Washing Shed, a corrugated iron building which was constructed in 1897. This building was demolished by London Transport in 1937 when the larger Met steam engines were transferred to the LNER. The LPTB built a small two-road brick engine shed to service the smaller Metropolitan engines which they retained. At the same time, the car sheds were completely rebuilt.

By 1924 the Neasden breakdown crane, of 10 tons capacity, was getting rather ancient and difficult to operate, and in October 1924 the Board authorised the purchase of a new breakdown crane from Cowans Sheldon & Co of Carlisle at a cost of £2,920. This could lift 20 tons at a radius of 20ft, or 15 tons at 25ft radius. It had a bogie at one end and 4 fixed wheels, which drove the crane when it was required to move, at the other. The new crane was delivered towards the end of 1925, and a second-hand match truck for use with it was purchased from the George Cohen & Armstrong Corporation for £55.

When electrification reached Harrow-on-the-Hill in 1905, the change-over from electric to steam traction was at first made at Wembley Park, but from 1st November 1906 this was moved to Harrow, where engine sidings and coaling and water facilities were provided. In 1925, after electric traction had been extended to Rickmansworth, similar facilities were provided there. At one time the transfer of the steam engine shed from Neasden to Rickmansworth was contemplated, but nothing came of this proposal.

When the Manchester, Sheffield & Lincolnshire (later Great Central) Railway was being extended to London over the Metropolitan tracks it was intended that the MSLR would purchase the Metropolitan works at Neasden, and the Met purchased a new site for workshops at Stoke Mandeville. Sir Edward Watkin, who was Chairman of both companies, doubtless favoured this arrangement, but he resigned through ill health in 1894, to be succeeded as Met Chairman by John Bell. Subsequently relations between the Metropolitan and the MSLR became very strained, and the latter company's purchase of Neasden Works never took place.

Holman F. Stephens, later a colonel and of light railway fame, was a pupil under Hanbury at Neasden in 1889-90. He gained experience as a fireman at the running shed in the Locomotive and Carriage Shops. It was possibly this connection which led to his later purchasing 19 'rigid-eight' coaches for his Burry Port & Gwendraeth Valley Railway and seven 'Jubilee' stock 4-wheelers for the Weston, Clevedon & Portishead Light Railway – the latter were still in existence when the line closed in 1940.

Henry Greenly became a junior engineering draughtsman at Neasden in 1897, and later assistant to the Surveyor and Architect. He left in 1901 and became famous as a designer and builder of miniature railways.

The Metropolitan breakdown crane at Neasden, 11th September 1926. This was purchased from Cowans, Sheldon & Co. in 1925 at a cost of £2,920. It could lift 20 tons at a radius of 20ft, or 15 tons at 25ft radius. The match truck was bought secondhand from the George Cohen & Armstrong Disposal Corporation. Both were withdrawn from service in the mid-1960s. LCGB Ken Nunn Collection

Appendix I
Locomotive Superintendents and CMEs

John Fowler

(Sir) John Fowler was Engineer to the Metropolitan Railway, being appointed in 1853. He supervised the construction of the railway, and was initially responsible for rolling stock. The 'hot brick' locomotive (see Chapter 1) was his idea. But he was not really a locomotive engineer, and when he ordered the 4-4-0 tank engines from Beyer Peacock he laid down only a broad specification for them, stipulating the diameter of the coupled wheels, weight per axle, and suitability for negotiating sharp curves.

Robert Harvey Burnett

A Beyer Peacock employee, Burnett played a part in the design of the Metropolitan 4-4-0 tank engines, and in 1862 he went to Spain to supervise the erection of eight 4-4-0 tank locomotives which Beyers were building for the Tudela & Bilbao Railway, and on which the Met design was broadly based. He was appointed Resident Engineer and Locomotive Superintendent of the Metropolitan on 20th April 1864 on Sir John Fowler's recommendation, at a salary of £300 per annum, increased to £500 on 1st January 1866. In 1872 the Met Board initiated an inquiry into the affairs of the Locomotive Department; it was felt that savings could be effected in the cost of repairs and renewals, and they called for a report on these and how many superfluous locomotives there were. The Board evidently considered that Burnett had been negligent and extravagant, and he was given three months notice in May 1872. In fairness to Burnett, however, it should be pointed out that until 1871 the Met had worked the District's trains as well as their own; the assumption of this task by the District with their own locomotives in 1871 could not have been anticipated, and was bound to make some Met engines redundant. It is possible too, that Burnett's ordering of the five large 0-6-0 tank engines from the Worcester Engine Co for the St John's Wood extension also earned him displeasure, as it was soon found that the standard Beyer Peacock tank engines could handle the gradients on this line quite easily, and the 0-6-0 tanks were sold.

On leaving the Metropolitan Burnett returned to his old firm, Beyer Peacock, as Works Manager.

Joseph Tomlinson Jr.

Burnett was succeeded by Joseph Tomlinson, one-time Locomotive Superintendent of the Taff Vale Railway, whose appointment was confirmed by the Board on 30th October 1872; he took over, presumably in August of that year, at a salary of £600. By 1884 his salary had risen to £800, but he resigned on 8th April 1885. In the year ending 31st December 1884 there had been 27 engine failures or incidents, the worst of these being derailments of engines 47 and 23 on different occasions at Mansion House, causing delays of 78 and 93 minutes respectively. Sir Edward Watkin, the Metropolitan Chairman, wrote to Tomlinson in March 1885 about these incidents and the disorganisation they caused, and the latter's resignation may have been as a result of Watkin's letter.

J.J. Hanbury

Tomlinson's successor was J.J. Hanbury, who had been employed in the Midland Railway's Locomotive Dept at Derby; he was appointed on 6th May 1885 at a salary of £600 per annum. His coming did not, however, bring about any great improvement in locomotive performance; there were 34 engine failures between 1st December 1890 and 14th January 1891. In order to improve this situation, responsibility for permanent way, which had hitherto been the remit of the Locomotive Superintendent who had also been the Resident Engineer, was given to W.H. Gates from 1st December 1891; he received the title Civil Engineer, leaving Hanbury to concentrate on locomotive matters. Hanbury resigned on 1st November 1893, and T.F. Raney, of the Carriage & Wagon Dept, was put in temporary charge of the Locomotive Dept at a salary of £4-10-0 per week, until a successor to Hanbury could be found.

When Alfred Watkin resigned as Locomotive Superintendent of the South Eastern Railway in September 1877 Tomlinson, then with the Metropolitan, and Hanbury, who was in Midland Railway employment, were among those interviewed for the South Eastern post, but both were unsuccessful, and James Stirling, of the Glasgow & South Western, was appointed as the SER's new Locomotive Superintendent.

T.F. Clark

At the end of 1893 the Met Board appointed T.F. Clark, the locomotive foreman at Neasden, as the new Locomotive Superintendent. When he resigned on 31st December 1905 his salary was £400 per annum, only half of what Hanbury was receiving when he left in 1893. Clark was paid a gratuity of £500 'in consideration of the circumstances under which it had been necessary for him to sever his connection with the Company', which suggests that illness was to blame for his resignation.

Charles Jones

By September 1905 all the Metropolitan lines south of Harrow-on-the-Hill had been electrified. Charles Jones had been Electrical Engineer since 1903, and on 1st January 1906 he was appointed Chief Resident Electrical & Mechanical Engineer. His first nine months in this post may have been a probationary period, as his salary was not increased until 1st September, when it became £850 per annm. Perhaps because of the growing importance of electric traction, the Board decided on 31st May 1923 to separate the functions of Chief Electrical and Chief Mechanical Engineer. The latter role would be combined with that of Works Manager at Neasden. Jones retired as Chief Electrical Engineer in mid-1924 due to ill-health, but his services were retained as a consultant for three more years.

George Hally

Selbie, the General Manager, interviewed six candidates for the post of Chief Mechanical Engineer, and he recommended George Hally, of Watford, who was appointed from 1st July 1923 at a salary of £1,200, increasing to £1,400 after 12 months if his work was satisfactory. He was also Traffic Manager from 1930, and when the Metropolitan was absorbed by London Transport on 1st July 1933 his salary was £3,000.

In looking back over these careers, it seems fair to say that its Locomotive Superintendents and CMEs managed to provide the Metropolitan with a reasonably efficient fleet of engines, though several classes, for example the Beyer Peacock 4-4-0 tanks, the Stirling-derived 'C' Class 0-4-4Ts, and the adapted Maunsell 'K' Class 2-6-4 tanks, were not original designs. The 0-6-4 and 4-4-4 tank engines were based on specifications from the Metropolitan and detailed design was left to the builders, but the performance of the whole fleet in service showed that the MET CME was aware of what the requirements of the situation were and knew how to provide for them.

Appendix II
Locomotive Liveries

Beyer Peacock 4-4-0T (built 1864-1885)

From 1864 to 1885 these were bright olive green, lined on boiler bands and side tanks with a yellow band and black lines, and with a yellow line on the inside of the wheel rims. Side tanks were lined with a small central panel, within which was mounted the Beyer Peacock works plate, and a larger panel on each side. Chimneys were copper capped and domes polished brass; the first 18 engines carried names on plates fixed to the boilers, but these were soon removed. The number was borne in brass figures on the front of the chimneys. A photograph of No.45, built in 1879, shows the side tanks lined in three *equal-sized* panels, with the works plate in the centre. The caption to this view, which appeared in the 'Railway Magazine' in 1908, says "No.45 . . . showing the modifications introduced by Mr. Tomlinson". (Tomlinson was Locomotive Superintendent from 1872 to 1885.)

In 1885 J.J. Hanbury came from the Midland Railway to become Locomotive Superintendent of the Metropolitan, and the colour changed to dark red (deeper than Midland red); this was known as Midcared, and remained the standard colour for Met steam locomotives for the rest of the company's existence, being perpetuated by London Transport after 1933. Under Hanbury the side tanks were lined in one panel only, with a black line edged with yellow, and still bore no evidence of ownership, carrying only the works plate in the centre; dome covers were painted over, but polished engine numbers still appeared on the chimneys; they were still carried by some engines as late as 1911.

When T.F. Clark took over as Locomotive Superintendent in 1893 he changed to lining the side tanks in three equal-sized panels, with 'Metropolitan Railway' in serif letters within two oval lines surrounding the engine number. The lining was black and yellow as before, and also appeared on the sides and back of the bunkers; a single yellow line was on the front and rear spectacle plates, on the cylinders and the rims of the wheels. Boiler bands were black and yellow; the engine number was painted in large numerals on the backs of the bunkers, and the letters 'M.R.' appeared in serif capitals on the buffer beams.

A London Transport photograph of No.27 (undated, but probably taken after 1918, as the engine carries tripcock apparatus), shows the side tanks lined in a single panel, with 'Metropolitan Railway' in small block capitals on either side of the crest. The running number was in small figures on the side of the bunker, and still appeared on the chimney, but painted over. By this time the Beyer tanks had mostly been reboilered with closed domes, and these were no longer polished, but painted. This may have been a transitional painting style; it is the only photograph I have seen showing this type of lettering, though an F. Moore coloured postcard shows 'E' class 0-4-4T No.81 similarly lettered.

When Charles Jones became Chief Mechanical Engineer in 1906 he introduced the final livery, red with lining as before, but with single-panel lining on the side tanks. The engine number usually appeared in large numerals below the word 'Metropolitan' which was in large capitals on the side tanks, but some locomotives had the number on the bunker side (No.41 is shown in photographs in both these styles). The number also appeared in large numerals on the back of the bunker, on the side of which some engines carried the Metropolitan crest. Lining of cab, cylinders and wheels was unchanged, with a single yellow line; boiler bands and the back of the bunkers had black and yellow lining. When the surviving Metropolitan steam locomotives were renumbered by London Transport in 1937, No.23, the only remaining 4-4-0 tank, carried its new number, L45, high on the cab side sheets, the position where its old number had been worn. It was lettered 'London Transport'.

'C' Class 0-4-4T (built 1891)

These originally had three-panel lining with the oval scroll showing 'Metropolitan Railway' surrounding the number – the latter also appeared on the chimney in brass figures, at least as late as 1911. But a later, though undated, London Transport photograph shows No.68 in the later style with single-panel lining and 'Metropolitan' on the side tank with the number below; the crest appeared on the bunker side.

'D' Class 2-4-0T (built 1894-95)

These engines originally had 3-panel lining and lettering as on the 'C' Class above, but with 'M.R.' in serif figures on the buffer beams. No.71 in 1916 and No.76 in 1920 had single panel lining with 'Metropolitan' on the side tanks and the number in *small* figures below, and this is probably the style in which all the 'D' Class engines finished up.

'E' Class 0-4-4T (built 1896-1901)

These engines were originally turned out with three-panel lining on the side tanks, but no lettering or number; this lining was rather more elaborate than before, the corners being as illustrated below, instead of the radiused corners used previously. Cast oval number plates with the number in raised

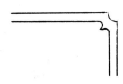

figures, surrounded by 'Metropolitan Railway' were carried on the bunker sides, and the number also appeared on the back of the bunker, e.g., 'No.77'. The original Metropolitan crest, which showed the back of a receding train, and the front of an approaching steam train, in twin tunnels, surmounted by the City of London arms and surrounded by an ornate design of scrolls and flowers, appeared on sandboxes. Later, the 'E' Class had single panel lining on the side tanks, with 'Metropolitan' in the centre, either with the number in small figures below, or on the side of the bunker. Boiler bands were black with yellow edging, and the backs of the bunkers were similarly lined. Footplate edging, axle ends and wheel rims and cab side sheets had a single yellow line, as did the splashers and sandboxes. Brass beading on splashers was originally polished brass, as were the domes, though both these features were later painted over. Numbers were painted in large figures on the back of the bunkers.

Peckett 0-6-0T (built 1897-1899)

Originally these engines had 3-panel lining, with the 'Metropolitan Railway' oval scroll surrounding the number. Later this gave way to a single panel on the saddle tanks with 'Metropolitan' in the centre; the number appeared high up on the side of the cab. Cab side sheets below waist level and the back of the bunker had double yellow lining; toolboxes, sandboxes, footplate edging and wheels had a single yellow line.

'F' Class 0-6-2T (built 1901)

The original lining and livery for these four locomotives was the same as described for the 'E' Class, and the later simpler style also followed that used on the 'E' Class. 'M.R.' was painted on the front buffer beams in earlier years.

'G' Class 0-6-4T, 'H' Class 4-4-4T and 'K' Class 2-6-4T

In their earlier years, the 'G' and 'H' Class engines had 'Metropolitan' and 'Railway' in curved lines (but not within a scroll) on the side tanks, with the later Metropolitan crest in the centre. Later the single word 'Metropolitan' replaced this, and this style was used on the 'K' Class from the outset. All three classes had plain brass number plates on the sides of the bunkers. Lining on tanks, boiler bands, cab side sheets and the sides and backs of bunkers was in black with yellow edging; similar lining was applied to the cylinders on the 'H' and 'K' Classes. Footplate edging and the rims and centres of wheels had a single yellow line, and the engine numbers appeared on front buffer beams. These numbers were also painted in figures about 18in tall on the back of bunkers; a photograph of 'H' Class No.103 when new shows these as shaded figures, but later, unshaded figures were used. The 'H' Class originally carried large oval Kerr Stuart works plates on the smokebox saddles, but these were later replaced by smaller plates.

Miscellaneous Locomotives

No photographs of the four 0-6-0 tank engines built by the Worcester Engine Co seem to exist showing them while still in Metropolitan ownership, but they were presumably painted green. The two Manning Wardle 0-6-0 saddle tanks acquired from the Oxford & Aylesbury Tramroad when the Met took over working of the Brill branch were apparently painted dark red with black bands and yellow edging on saddle tanks and cab sides, and a single yellow line on cab fronts and the front of the saddle tanks. They did not carry the 'Metropolitan' lettering.

General

In their later days all Metropolitan engines had their class letter painted in small letters under the running number, on side tanks and on backs of bunkers.

When the LPTB took over in 1933 they retained the Metropolitan dark red livery and lining, but engines were lettered 'London Transport', and on the three larger classes the original style of running numbers on the back of the bunkers was replaced by numerals of standard Johnston type. These numbers were also painted on front and rear buffer beams. In the early days of the Board's ownership at least two locomotives, 'F' Class No.91 and 'H' Class No.105, were lettered 'MET.'; these were probably repainted thus as a temporary measure while the LPTB decided what fleet name to adopt – they did not use 'London Transport' until about mid-1934.

The 'G', 'H' and 'K' Classes were all transferred to the LNER in 1937 and retained their Met numbers until then; after overhaul at Stratford Works they emerged in unlined LNER black livery. The smaller engines retained by the Board received new numbers in the series L45 to L54, and these numbers appeared below 'London Transport' on the side tanks.

Appendix III
Disposal of Beyer Peacock 4-4-0 Tank Engines

Engine	Date	
*1	1897	Withdrawn after damage in accident at Baker Street
2	1907	Sold to R. Fraser & Sons, Newcastle-on-Tyne (scrap merchants)
3	1907	Sold to R. Fraser for £290
4/5/6	1907	Sold to R. Fraser; No.6 resold to Pelaw Main Colliery, 1926
7	1925	Sold to R. Fraser; resold to Mersey Railway to replace Metropolitan No.61
8	1907	Sold to R. Fraser
9	1906	Sold to R. Fraser for £252-10-0
10/11/12	1905	Sold to Cambrian Railways for £550 each
13	1905	Sold to Cambrian Railways for £550
14	1905	Sold to South Hetton Coal Co for £700
15	1905	Sold to Cambrian Railways for £500
16	1907	Sold to R. Fraser for £290
17	1907	Sold to R. Fraser
18	1928	Sold to Sir Arthur Elvin, proprietor of Wembley Stadium for £190.
19	1911	Sold to R. Fraser for £166-10-0
20	1905	Sold to Bradford Corporation for £625
21	1906	Sold to R. Fraser for £252-10-0

Cambrian Railways 4-4-0T No.12, formerly Met A Class No.11, at Barmouth. After electrification, the Metropolitan sold six 4-4-0 tanks, Nos.10-13, 15 and 66, to the Cambrian in 1905-07. All six passed into Great Western ownership in 1922 (by this time two had been rebuilt as 4-4-0 tender engines) but were scrapped before receiving the GWR numbers (1113-14 and 1129-32) allotted to them. This photograph shows the engine as fitted with a cab, of Metropolitan pattern, and with the condensing gear removed — these appear to be the only alterations made by its new owners. L&GRP

A *Class* 4-4-0T L45 (Met No.23) at Neasden in October 1958 and in May 1963 after restoration for the Underground Centenary Parade. The locomotive had been withdrawn from service in 1948. Photomatic/H. Clarke

Engine	Date	
*22	1925	Sold to District Railway for £300 (District No.L35)
23	1948	Withdrawn as London Transport L45; restored, and preserved at Covent Garden Museum
24	1913	Sold to R. Fraser; resold to Birtley Colliery 1922
25	1913	Sold to R. Fraser
26	1926	Sold to Pelaw Main Colliery; scrapped 1948
27	1935	Sold
28	1906	Sold to Sherwood Colliery
29	1925	Scrapped at Neasden
30	1907	Sold to R. Fraser for £290
31/32	1906	Sold to R. Fraser for £252-10-0 each
33	1907	Sold to R. Fraser for £235
34	1905	Sold to Bradford Corporation for £625
35/36	1906	Sold to R. Fraser for £217-10-0 each
37	1907	Sold, via A. King & Co, to West Somerset Mineral Railway for £400
38	1907	Sold to R. Fraser for £290
39	1906	Sold to R. Fraser for £252
40	1907	Sold to R. Fraser for £235
41	1936	Scrapped at Neasden
42	1925	Sold to R. Fraser
43	1913	Sold to R. Fraser
44	1925	Sold to R. Fraser; resold to Pelaw Main Colliery 1926, scrapped 1948
45	1906	Sold to R. Fraser for £252-10-0
46	1928	Sold to Sir Arthur Elvin for £190
47	1906	Sold to R. Fraser for £252-10-0
48	1936	Sold
49	1936	Scrapped
50	1907	Sold to R. Fraser for £290
51	1911	Sold to R. Fraser for £160
52/53	1907	Sold to R. Fraser for £290 each
54/55	1906	Sold to R. Fraser for £217-10-0 each
56	1907	Sold to R. Fraser
57	1907	Sold to R. Fraser for £290
58/59	1911	Sold to R. Fraser for £160 each
60	1907	Sold to R. Fraser for £290
61	1907	Sold to Mersey Railway for £666 after repairs; scrapped 1925 and replaced by No.7
62/63	1907	Sold to R. Fraser for £290 each
64	1907	Sold to R. Fraser
65	1911	Sold to R. Fraser for £160
66	1905	Sold to Cambrian Railways for £500

* No.22 was fitted for oil burning in October 1921, but this equipment had been removed prior to sale

Some of the engines purchased by R. Fraser & Sons in 1906-07 were cut up at Neasden by them.

The two locomotives purchased by Bradford Corporation in 1905 were for use on the Nidd Valley Light Railway, which served their reservoir at Angram. This line, which joined the North Eastern Railway branch from Nidd Junction at Pateley Bridge, was opened in 1907. From 1905 until the line was opened they presumably were used on constructing the railway. They were given heavy repairs at Neasden and the condensing apparatus was removed before sale; at the same time Neasden repainted them, still in the dark red Metropolitan colour, but with three-panel lining on the side tanks. They had the locomotive's name in an arc over the Bradford coat of arms in the centre panel, flanked by 'Bradford' and 'Corporation' on the panels to the left and right. Brass number plates appeared on the bunker sides.

No.20 ('A' Class) built 1866, became Nidd Valley No.1 'Holdsworth'.

No.34 ('B' Class) built 1879, became Nidd Valley No.2 'Milner'.

'Holdsworth' was scrapped by the Corporation in about 1920, but 'Milner' was resold in 1914 and worked for a few more years at the Conway Quarry, North Wales, where it was renamed 'Conway'.

Ex-Metropolitan *B Class* 4-4-0T No.37 at Watchet on the re-opening of the West Somerset Mineral Railway, 4th July 1907. The WSMR was originally opened between 1857 and 1864 to serve iron ore mines in the Brendon Hills; the mines closed down in 1879, though a passenger service on the railway continued until 1898. In 1907 the Somerset Minerals Syndicate purchased No.37 for £400 when they re-opened two of the mines and the railway. The venture was not a success, however, and it collapsed in 1910. No.37 was sold by auction, and the purchaser may have been the Bute Works Supply Co, but this is not known for certain. Author's Collection

Nidd Valley Light Railway 4-4-0T No.1 'Holdsworth', formerly Met *A Class* No.20. This engine and *B Class* No.34 were sold to Bradford Corporation in 1905 for use on the Nidd Valley line, which served their reservoir at Angram. They were given a heavy overhaul at Neasden before disposal and repainted in Met. dark red, but lettered as shown. No.20 was scrapped in about 1920, but No.34, which became Nidd Valley No.2 'Milner', was resold in 1914 to the Conway Quarry in North Wales. L&GRP

Appendix IV
The Enginemen

Having described the locomotives, some notes on the men who drove and fired them may be of interest. Like all enginemen, they were a hardy breed; in 1897 one driver had been at work for 33 years, and another had joined the company 24 years earlier as cleaner; the sulphurous atmosphere of the tunnels did not seem to be harmful to their health. For most of the time that the Beyer Peacock 4-4-0 tanks were working on the Aylesbury line they were without cabs, but even winter weather was cheerfully accepted by these Spartan characters – indeed, when both the Metropolitan and the District first proposed to fit cabs, the enginemen rejected them as making work in the underground sections too hot for comfort.

Their hours were long and arduous; in the 1870s the first Metropolitan locomotive to leave the depot did so at 5.15am and the last one returned at 1.15am. Enginemen worked for eight or nine hours at a stretch and had to take their meals on the footplate while their trains were on the move, as there was little time to eat at the longer station stops when the engines had to be serviced. In 1871 the basic working week for enginemen was reduced from 57½ to 54 hours and remained at that figure in the 1890s, when overtime was paid at time and a quarter. At this time a Metropolitan driver was earning 6s to 8s per day, and a fireman 3s 6d to 4s 6d, which compared quite well with the pay of London bus and tramway staff.

When the locomotive works and sheds were moved to Neasden in the early 1880s, the Metropolitan built houses for its employees, known as Neasden Village. Sir Edward Watkin, the Met Chairman, took the enlightened view that although the company might lose a small proportion of its capital by so doing, it would attract "a better class of workman". He said "My experience is that we gain indirectly a great benefit by practically improving the comfort of the people whom we employ". This housing consisted of two parallel streets, 'A Street' with 62 cottages and 'B Street' with 40. These were renamed Quainton Street and Verney Street in the early 1900s, and Aylesbury Street comprising 40 more cottages was opened in 1905. The Village also contained shops and two missions to look after the spiritual needs of Met employees, and in 1883 St Saviour's Church was built with a small school adjoining it. Free uniforms and free travel to and from work were also provided, of course, so in many ways Metropolitan enginemen were quite well looked after.

When electric traction began in 1905 many enginemen were trained as motormen, and the theory was taught at the General Training School which was established within the Neasden Works. Actual driving instruction was given on the Rayners Lane to South Harrow spur line.

Quainton Street, Neasden in 1988. Originally designated 'A' Street when built in 1882 to accommodate staff at the then new Neasden Works and Depot, this consisted of 62 cottages; the parallel 'B' Street (Verney Street from 1903) had 40 cottages of slightly different design. Ten shops were also provided, though only five of these found tenants, and the remainder were converted into dwellings in 1889. A further 40 cottages (Aylesbury Street) were added in 1904-06, and between 1924 and 1927 a total of 202 cottages, semi-detached and including some which were of an unusual reinforced concrete design, were built.
Author

Appendix V
Metropolitan Railway Opening Dates

January 10th 1863	Paddington (GWR, Bishops Road) – Farringdon Street
June 13th 1864	Hammersmith & City Railway – Hammersmith – Bishops Road (Joint with GWR)
July 1st 1864	Latimer Road (H&CR) – Uxbridge Road Junction (West London Railway)
December 23rd 1865	Farringdon Street – Moorgate
March 1st 1866	Widened Lines, Farringdon Street – Aldersgate & Barbican
July 1st 1866	Widened Lines, Aldersgate – Moorgate
April 13th 1868	Baker Street – Swiss Cottage (Metropolitan & St Johns Wood Railway)
February 2nd 1868	Commencement of Great Northern Railway service, Kings Cross to Farringdon Street, over Widened Lines
July 13th 1868	Junction with Midland Railway and Widened Lines brought into use
October 1st 1868	Praed Street Junction (Paddington) – Gloucester Road
December 24th 1868	Gloucester Road – South Kensington
September 1st 1871	Junction with London, Chatham & Dover Railway (Snow Hill Junction) to Smithfield in use for LCDR service into Moorgate
February 1st 1875	Moorgate – Liverpool Street (Great Eastern Railway)
July 12th 1875	Liverpool Street Metropolitan station opened
November 18th 1876	Liverpool Street – Aldgate
June 30th 1879	Swiss Cottage – West Hampstead
November 24th 1879	West Hampstead – Willesden Green
August 2nd 1880	Willesden Green – Harrow-on-the-Hill
October 1st 1880	Junction with Midland Railway at Finchley Road
September 25th 1882	Aldgate – Tower Hill (temporary station)
October 6th 1884	Inner Circle completed: Tower Hill – Mansion House (Joint with District Railway from Aldgate to Mansion House); curve Aldgate to Aldgate East; Aldgate to Whitechapel and junction with East London Railway (joint with District Railway); Metropolitan service Hammersmith to New Cross (South Eastern Railway) over East London Railway
May 25th 1885	Harrow-on-the-Hill – Pinner
September 1st 1887	Pinner – Rickmansworth
July 8th 1889	Rickmansworth – Chesham
July 1st 1891	Aylesbury & Buckingham Railway (Aylesbury to Verney Junction (LNWR) absorbed by the Metropolitan
September 1st 1892	Chalfont & Latimer (junction with Chesham line) – Aylesbury (temporary Met station)
January 1st 1894	Aylesbury Joint Station opened, and junction with Great Western Railway
July 26th 1898	Junction with Great Central Railway at Quainton Road brought into use by GCR coal trains. Two tracks for exclusive use of GCR from Finchley Road (Canfield Place) to Preston Road
March 15th 1899	Great Central Railway passenger trains to Marylebone, using Met tracks south of Quainton Road
December 1st 1899	Quainton Road to Brill branch leased by Metropolitan
July 4th 1904	Harrow-on-the-Hill – Uxbridge (Steam trains)
January 1st 1905	Electric trains Baker Street to Uxbridge
July 1st 1905	Electric working, Aldgate to South Kensington (partial)
September 24th 1905	Electric working on Inner Circle service
April 2nd 1906	Metropolitan & Great Central Railway Joint Committee formed, and takes over operation of Harrow South Junction – Verney Junction, and Chesham and Brill branches
December 2nd 1906	Withdrawal of Met steam trains over East London Railway
March 31st 1913	Metropolitan electric trains over East London Railway to New Cross (SER) and New Cross (LBSCR)
July 1st 1913	Great Northern & City Railway (Moorgate to Finsbury Park) acquired by Metropolitan
January 5th 1925	Electric traction Harrow-on-the-Hill – Rickmansworth
November 2nd 1925	Moor Park/Rickmansworth – Watford (Metropolitan and LNER Joint). Electric traction, also LNER steam trains initially, but these were withdrawn on the outbreak of the General Strike on May 4th 1926, and never resumed on a regular basis
December 10th 1932	Wembley Park – Stanmore

The Harrow-on-the-Hill – Uxbridge branch was not included in the Metropolitan & Great Central Joint Committee, and the Stanmore branch was a purely Metropolitan line, without LNER participation.

Appendix VI
The Preservation of E Class Tank No.1

It may be of interest to recount how 0-4-4 tank No.1, the only preserved Metropolitan Railway steam locomotive still in working order, came to be saved from the scrap-heap and restored.

As mentioned in Chapter 6, No.1 was built by the Metropolitan themselves at Neasden in 1898, one of three engines of this class constructed there to the design of T.F. Clark, the Met Locomotive Superintendent. Together with a further four E Class engines built by Hawthorn Leslie, these rather handsome 0-4-4 tanks were the Metropolitan's top link locomotives for passenger trains on the Extension Line until the appearance of the G Class 0-6-4Ts in 1915/16; even then, the E Class continued to be used on these duties until the H Class 4-4-4 tanks arrived in 1920. No.1 itself had its moment of glory on July 4th 1904 when, lavishly decorated with flowers and bunting, it hauled the special train for the opening of the Uxbridge branch. Among its later regular duties was that of hauling the Chesham branch train, usually consisting of two 'Dreadnought' coaches, and this task continued until 1937 when LNER locomotives took over this working.

On July 1st 1933 the Metropolitan Railway was absorbed by the London Passenger Transport Board. Four years later the E Class were renumbered, and No.1 became London Transport L44. Its dark red livery was unchanged, apart from the substitution of 'London Transport' for 'Metropolitan' on its side tanks. By 1941 the only survivors of the seven E Class engines were L44, L46 (Met No.77) and L48 (Met No.81). By this time they were chiefly employed on engineering trains, but in the postwar years, when Neasden LNER engine shed was very short of motive power (the LNER having taken over the working of all Metropolitan Line steam trains in 1937) one of the E Class used to stand by in the bay platform at Rickmansworth, and occasionally had the honour of taking over haulage of a train onwards to Aylesbury.

Also during the postwar period, L44 was employed on several special trains. On July 4th 1954 it worked the 50th anniversary special on the Uxbridge branch, a duty which, as already noted, it had performed on the opening train in 1904. The 'Railway World Special' to Chesham, on May 22nd 1955, saw L44 in action once again, and a Southern Counties Touring Society excursion on October 1st 1961 included a working to New Cross Gate, Southern Region, probably the first occasion on which an E Class engine had visited the East London Line.

By the late 1950s the surviving Met steam locomotives were nearing the end of their useful lives. The possibility of renewing the E Class and the F Class 0-6-2 tanks with boilers from ex-South Eastern & Chatham H Class 0-4-4Ts was considered, but nothing came of this, and trials with a BR 350hp diesel-electric shunter were unsuccessful. But in 1955 Western Region 57XX class 0-6-0 pannier tank No.7711 was tested, and proved much more effective; between then and 1963 twelve more engines of this type were acquired. The last of these was withdrawn in 1971, and this marked the end of steam on London Transport railways.

This resulted in E Class L46 being withdrawn in 1962, but L44 and L48 survived for another year. L44 appeared in the parade at Neasden in May 1963 to mark the centenary of the Metropolitan Railway, and was also used, together with L48, at Moorgate in the following week, in connection with a re-enactment of the well-known photograph showing VIPs travelling in contractor's wagons on the Metropolitan in May 1862, before the opening of the line.

After this, L44 was sold to the London Railway Preservation Society, forerunner of the Quainton Railway Society. At this time, the LRPS had no permanent home, and L44 was eventually delivered to an industrial site in Luton. Here the engine was steamed on several occasions and, under the watchful eye of an ex-BR fireman, members enjoyed their first taste of footplate life. Later L44 was moved to a location in the Bedford area. While there, the LRPS was invited to display L44 in steam at Bedford St Johns station; at that time, the only engine officially allowed to travel in steam over BR tracks was No.4472 'Flying Scotsman'. Work began to prepare the locomotive for public exhibition, and a BR boilersmith gave up his spare time to help the LRPS, as a new boiler certificate was required.

Morale was high at this time with everybody working flat out, but with just days to go the workforce suffered a great disappointment when the BR management decided that the steam ban could not be lifted.

E Class 0-4-4T No.1 on special train for the Chesham branch centenary, at Watford, July 8th 1989. The train consisted, rather incongruously, of a Network SouthEast 4-VEP electric unit and a BR Mark 1 standard coach, with electric locomotive No.12, 'Sarah Siddons', bringing up the rear. Metropolitan No.1 and other members of the E Class were regular performers on the Chesham branch in Met and early London Transport days. It is now preserved at the Quainton Railway Society. This was probably the first visit of an E Class engine to Watford.
Frank Goudie

There was now no urgency to return the engine to working condition and, still with its hydraulic test blanking plates in position, it was moved to a private siding in the Aylesbury area – back onto home territory. Meanwhile, the Quainton Railway Society was being formed to purchase the redundant station and sidings at Quainton Road, later developed as the Quainton Railway Centre. This was to be L44's permanent home, and a final journey was made up the Met & GC main line, together with an LNWR 12-wheel dining car and three Midland wagons.

The engine was still in need of boiler attention and, as there were other locomotives which could be more easily restored to working order, it was stored until 1975, when a hydraulic test showed that fairly major work was now needed on the boiler. The decision was taken that L44 should receive a major overhaul, and this task was in hand by 1976, but progress was slow in view of other commitments. However, 1979 saw the frames united with the driving wheels and bogie, and attention had been given to the axleboxes, horns and other running gear. De-scaling and painting were also involved; it had been decided to return L44 to the deep crimson Metropolitan livery as Met No.1.

But, once again, circumstances were to delay the return to service of the veteran. Ex-GWR 57XX 0-6-0PT No.7715, in itself an ex-LT machine, was in need of major attention, and for various reasons it was decided to proceed with its overhaul before that of Met No.1. And so for the next four years the boilerless frames languished at the end of the shed while No.7715 was completely rebuilt.

Restoration work was eventually resumed, however, and completed during 1986. Resplendent in dark red livery and with its old number, Metropolitan No.1 won the National Coal Board Steam Heritage Award for 1987, and was on loan for a while to the Mid-Hants Railway.

Two years later it returned to its old happy hunting ground, the Chesham branch, when on the weekends of July 8th/9th and 15th/16th July 1989 it hauled special trains to commemorate the centenary of the branch. The coaching stock used for these workings was, rather incongruously, a Network SouthEast Class 423 (4 VEP) 4-car electric unit and a BR Mark 1 coach, with Met. No.1 at the 'country' end and electric locomotive No.12 'Sarah Siddons' at the other end. The train ran between Chesham and Watford. No.1 looked very smart indeed, and it is very good to know that this veteran Metropolitan Railway locomotive is once more in fine working order.

For much of the information on which this appendix is based I am indebted to an article in 'Railway World' for June 1984 by Mr T.J. Page of the Quainton Railway Society.

Bibliography

Metropolitan Railway Board Minute Books

Metropolitan Railway Stores Committee Minute Books

'The Early Locomotive History of the Metropolitan Railway', articles by A. Rosling Bennett, 'Railway Magazine', 1908

'The Engines of the St. John's Wood Railway', article by H.H. Annand, S.L.S Journal, September 1967

'Locomotive and Train Working in the latter half of the 19th Century' article by E.L. Ahrons, 'Railway Magazine', December 1924

'Engines of the Metropolitan Railway sold to Industrial Users', article by G. Alliez, 'Railway Observer', November 1940

'London Transport – its Locomotives' by P. Densham, 1947

'A History of London Transport' by T.C. Barker and Michael Robbins, Volume II, (George Allen & Unwin)

'London's Metropolitan Railway' by Alan A. Jackson (David & Charles)

'The Last Drop' by John Day and William Fenton (London Transport)

'The Great Central in LNER Days' by D. Jackson and Owen Russell (Ian Allan)

'The Wotton Tramway (Brill Branch)' by Ken Jones (Oakwood Press)

Profile No.10 'The Met. Tanks' by Brian Reed (Profile Publications)

'The Locomotives of the South Eastern Railway' by D. Bradley (RCTS)

'The Story of London's Underground' by John R. Day (London Transport)

'Metropolitan No.1' article by T.J. Page, 'Railway World', June 1984, and letter from C.H. Gooch, 'Railway World' October 1984

'Locomotives of the LNER' Parts 7 and 9A (RCTS)

'Some Notes on the Yorkshire Engine Company,' article by C.B. Harley, SLS Journal, March 1976

'The "Beyer" 4-4-0 Metropolitan Tank Locomotives', articles by K.A.C.R. Nunn, SLS Journal, 1942/43

'The Metro-Land Tanks' article by Philip Atkins, 'Railways South East' Winter 1987/88

'The Metropolitan Railway and the Making of Neasden' by Robert Barker (Brent Leisure)

'Minor Railways of England and their Locomotives' by George Woodcock (Goose & Son, Norwich)

'The Later Days of Metropolitan Steam' by H.C. Casserley (Bradford Barton)

'Steam to Silver' by J. Graeme Bruce, Second Edition (Capital Transport)

'Workhorses of the London Underground' by J. Graeme Bruce (Capital Transport)

'The Old Mineral Line' by R.J. Sellick (Exmoor Press)

Records of locomotives repaired at Neasden Works, 1900-1937 (held at National Railway Museum, York).

London & North Eastern Railway Board Minutes and Secretarial Papers.